PATHWAYS TO FAMILY MYTHS

PATHWAYS TO FAMILY MYTHS

By

Vimala Pillari, D.S.W.

BRUNNER/MAZEL, *Publishers* • New York

Library of Congress Cataloging in Publication Data

Pillari, Vimala.
  Pathways to family myths.

  Bibliography: p. 181.
  Includes index.
  1. Aged—United States—Interviews. 2. Life
cycle, Human—Case studies. 3. Family—United
States—Case studies. I. Title. II. Title: Family
myths.
HQ1064.U5P55 1986   305.2'6   85-29096
ISBN 0-87630-401-3

Copyright © 1986 by Vimala Pillari

Published by
BRUNNER/MAZEL, INC.
19 Union Square West
New York, New York 10003

MANUFACTURED IN THE UNITED STATES OF AMERICA

Dedicated to
Father
(who is no more)
Mother
my grandparents
and
five generations of great grandparents
whose real history and mythology
gave us a special family culture

Acknowledgments

First of all I would like to express my deep gratitude to all the interviewees in the study for giving me permission for their material to be published. In all cases the names have been changed and the study is published with respect and understanding. My heartfelt thanks go to the four people who willingly participated in the long-term study and revealed their life stories to me. I express my deep gratitude to them for the hours they spent with me and for giving me insights into relationships. My special thanks go to the administrators of this large agency within western New York for allowing us to conduct the research at our own pace and on our own terms.

I am greatly indebted to my colleagues at the State University of New York at Buffalo: to Don Andersen, the Research Investigator, for his dedicated work; to Isaac Alcabes, who patiently read the chapters and constructively critiqued them; to Gerald Miller and David Kaye for their initial help on the project; to interim Dean, Hugh Petri, for his concern, interest, and support. At the Norfolk State University, my special thanks to Dean Moses Newsome for his complete support.

To Ann Alhadeff, of Brunner/Mazel publishers, my thanks for her understanding support and masterful guidance.

V. P.

Foreword

How families construct the experience of their reality—their family myths—has long been central to theories of family therapy and family dysfunction. For example, the myths of harmony to which colleagues and I applied the label of pseudomutuality (Wynne et al., 1958) was hypothesized to be "a major feature of the kind of setting in which reactive schizophrenia develops when other factors are also present" (p. 208). We observed that the shared family perception of omnipresent harmony can be maintained, despite observable conflictual behavior, through "the creation of a pervasive familial subculture of myths, legends, and ideology which stress the catastrophic consequences of openly recognized divergence" (p. 211). In a similar manner, Ferreira (1963) and Stierlin (1973) emphasized the defensive and protective functions of myths for the family system.

In more recent years, the concept of family myths has received less attention in research and theory than the study of communication sequences and of changes in interaction with therapy. Some of this research, preoccupied with coding tape-recorded transactions, has neglected the important issue of congruence, or lack of it, between the family members' experience of themselves and the observer's view. Sluzki (1983) has suggested a corrective to this approach by proposing an integration of three core orientations to family therapy—those centered on the *processes* of family interaction, on family *structure*, especially family boundaries and hierarchies, and on the family's *"world view,"* that is, the mythology of "agreement about the order and meaning attributed to the events of joint experiences" (p. 473).

Insofar as these various formulations have been concerned with family therapy and, hence, with relief of family dysfunction, there has been an underemphasis upon the healthy functions served by family belief systems, upon the significance of myths in the "normal" cultural transmission of values and behavior guidelines. Vimala Pillari has provided a splendid deepening of our understanding of the development, perpetuation, and modification of family myths. Her methods of detailed, semi-structured interviewing with ordinary, working-class, elderly people bring to this field a broadened time perspective, and do not begin with the therapist's skewed attention to pathology.

In these pages, the reader will find many examples of marital and family dances or rituals. Myths vitalize rituals, give them metaphorical content and meaning, while rituals give concrete expression for experienced behavior. Rituals are nodal episodes that inform what one is expected to see as "reality" and are part of the more enduring aspects of family myths that explain a family or other group to itself and to others. If we examine the myths of our ancient history or of our paranoid patients and families, we can expect to find a kernel of truth in them. When in the 19th century, Heinrich Schliemann, the father of archeology, read Homer, he took it seriously, unlike people before him who thought Troy was a fiction, a fantasy. He went to look where the myths had suggested Troy might be, and he found it. When we use the word "myth," we are talking about beliefs, whether or not they are verifiable; they are beliefs that family therapists and family researchers alike will do well to respect for both their past and their current meaning and force. The ritualized prescriptions of Selvini-Palazzoli and her Milan colleagues (1978) illustrate the therapeutic application of this principle.

In giving attention to the positive as well as to the distorting functions of myths, the thinking of family therapists is becoming

consonant with the diversity of interpretations of myths by an-
thropologists, historians, and scholars over the millenia. Campbell (1949) has most eloquently described the broad implications
of Pillari's fascinating study of family myths:

> Mythology has been interpreted by modern intellect as a
> primitive, fumbling effort to explain the world of nature
> (Frazer); as a production of poetical fantasy from prehistoric
> times, misunderstood by succeeding ages (Muller); as a
> repository of allegorical instruction, to shape the individual
> to his group (Durkheim); as a group dream, symptomatic
> of archetypal urges within the depths of the human psyche
> (Jung); as the traditional vehicle of man's profoundest meta-
> physical insights (Coomaraswamy); and as God's Revelation
> to His children (the Church). Mythology is all of these. The
> various judgments are determined by the viewpoints of the
> judges. For when scrutinized in terms of not what it is but
> of how it functions, of how it has served mankind in the
> past, of how it may serve today, mythology shows itself to
> be as amenable as life itself to the obsessions and require-
> ments of the individual, the race, the age. (p. 382)

> Throughout the inhabited world, in all times and under
> every circumstance, the myths of man have flourished; and
> they have been the living inspiration of whatever else may
> have appeared out of the activities of the human body and
> mind. It would not be too much to say that myth is the secret
> opening through which the inexhaustible energies of the
> cosmos pour into human cultural manifestation. Religions,
> philosophies, arts, the social forms of primitive and historic
> man, prime discoveries in science and technology, the very
> dreams that blister sleep, boil up from the basic, magic ring
> of myth. (p. 3)

This volume opens up and enriches the work of family therapists by showing how myths help shape the family and the lives
of its members.

Lyman C. Wynne, M.D., Ph.D.

REFERENCES

Campbell, J. *The Hero with a Thousand Faces*. Princeton: Princeton University Press, 1949.

Ferreira, A. J. Family myth and homeostasis. *Archives of General Psychiatry*, 1963, 9, 457–463.

Selvini-Palazzoli, M., Boscolo, L., Cecchin, G., and Prata, G. A ritualized prescription in family therapy: Odd days and even days. *Journal of Marriage and Family Counseling*, 1978, 4, 3–9.

Sluzki, C. E. Process, structure and world views: Toward an integrated view of systemic models in family therapy. *Family Process*, 1983, 22, 469–476.

Stierlin, H. Group fantasies and family myths—Some theoretical and practical aspects. *Family Process*, 1973, 12, 111–125.

Wynne, L.C., Ryckoff, I.M., Day, J., and Hirsch, S.I. Pseudomutuality in the family relations of schizophrenics. *Psychiatry*, 1958, 21, 205–220.

Contents

Introduction

I became interested in family myths in the course of learning, practicing and teaching about family therapy. I found over and over that each family had its own culture that had a profound lifelong influence on the attitudes, behavior and relationships of its members. One aspect of this culture was a set of myths that tended to persist whether or not they were supported by objective reality.

I decided that one way to gain insight into the origin and development of these myths would be to study the evolution of family myths and their impact on the lives of elderly people. While the overwhelming majority of aged people live in their own homes or with relatives, I chose subjects who were living in an institution away from their families. These individuals had severed themselves from family living due to medical, social and economic circumstances. (Two of the subjects of the intensive case studies were living with their spouses in the institution.)

The primary aim of my investigation was to set forth a systematic conception of each person's entire life cycle while paying special attention to the major myths in his or her life, as manifested at different stages of development.

Do the old family myths still exist for these individuals in spite of new and very different living situations? How do they start in

families? Do the myths serve a purpose in maintaining the coherence of the family, and under what conditions? Do family
myths disintegrate and when does this happen? I hoped to find
some answers to my questions, though I was not sure, where
this would lead. Family myths, as a subject, are relatively unexplored. While I was thrilled and excited by the challenge, I found
it a long, uncharted journey, full of frustration and ambiguity.
On reflection, I know now the agony and the joy of discovery
were well worth the effort.

In this undertaking, 25 elderly people were studied by a team
of two people. These 25 people were interviewed for a period
ranging from three to four hours each. For case study purposes
I chose four elderly people: Two were currently married, one was
widowed and another was divorced. I made several visits to their
rooms and their recreational areas. At times I sat with them while
they ate their lunch, we talked, I listened and taped. The four
people studied more fully were interviewed at least five times;
the amount of time spent with each person varied between 12
to 15 hours, over a period of three and a half months. The identities of the individuals have been disguised but their life stories
have been presented from the respondents' perspective as told
to me. The analyses and interpretations are my own, teased out
from these life stories.

I have gathered my data through audiotaping interviews because it provided me an opportunity to listen and relisten to the
tapes. This seemed like an endless process. I found afternoon
turning to night, light into darkness, as I sat taking notes and
listening to the voices and stories of these people. It was useful
to relive my experience with these elderly people. It helped me
to go back and forth from writing to tapes as I developed insights
into family myths and related these factors to families I had studied. I plowed through books on anthropology, mythology, psychology, and sociology, as well as on family therapy, backing
my findings with relevant documentation.

Human life fills me with a potent, intoxicating curiosity. To
study these people, I had to see them before me; what I cannot
see as actuality and what I cannot hear as the sound from a par-

ticular voice do not appear to hold my interest. The result of my study is an account of disciplined interviewing combined with an attempt at multidimensional interpretation of life in its complexity.

In this book I try to demonstrate how an understanding of older people in their own life cycle provides insights into family myths. While relating their life story, the older person transforms himself or herself and reveals cycles of feelings ranging from love to anger, rage, and so forth. As Jules Henry (1965) says, life has an inner calculus, which is the passage of existence through time, through one state into another, by leaps and by bounds, from one theme to another, from one mood to another, from one person to another, from one embrace or struggle to another, to its final summation and final dissolution. But family myths do not end with the death of a person, they are passed on, like some precious treasure that is the birthright of a family, to be carried on, modified or destroyed.

THE STUDY OF FAMILY MYTHS

This book is a beginning . . . the beginning, I hope, of what will in the next few years become a description of the fundamental structure underlying family myths.

In my writing I am also concerned with the persons who are part of family myths. What people believe becomes a part of them so that, in time, it becomes difficult to separate the person from the myth. The family myths discussed in this book are the myths created by particular families. It is necessary to understand that each family, like each individual, is unique; each family creates its own myths.

The Complexity of Family Life

I believe no single piece of behavior can be considered in isolation. The significance of any single event can be evaluated only as part of a configuration of events. Possibly the main problem with which I have struggled was to put things together in order to be able to relate events to one another in context and in time. What I perceive one day and cannot pursue I take back to the person the next day for my clarification and understanding. In this process, we, the elderly person and I, reexperience an incident or part of the life history.

I do not believe that anything is "commonplace." All the apparent trivia of everyday life are significant to me, if for no reason than that the commonplace does tell something about what people take for granted. If an interviewee came out with a response like, "John was mama's favorite," and brushes it aside, a light goes on and I say, "Tell me more," even though everyone in that family knew, accepted and lived with this belief. It was commonplace to them; to me it was not and I pursued its trail fervently. Often, it seemed as if it was the commonplace that revealed most about family myths. I believe that science often advances by relentless reexamination of the commonplace. Some of the greatest discoveries have been made through fascination with what other people have regarded as unworthy of noting.

The Task of History

The task of history is to capture the system of interactions. As the German philosopher/historian Wilhelm Dilthey (1962) observed, the historian penetrates more deeply into the structure of the historical world by sorting out and studying individual contexts. The fundamental of these contexts is the course of an individual life in the environment by which it is affected and which it affects.

Historic family contexts express our time and culture and are themselves micro-movements in history. When we look at the lives of the four people studied in greater depth here, along with the myths that motivate them, we are struck by the ordinariness of lives that these people have created, endured and lived through. This is the key to understanding these individuals and their families and, to some extent, ourselves.

As my research progressed, it became increasingly clear to me that I needed to utilize a developmental approach. There was little existing theory and even less research evidence regarding family myths in the life cycle of a person.

My interest is in family myths as they evolve in studying the life course of a person. This requires us to place the individual in the environment and examine his or her involvements in the world as well as fantasies that the person has about conflicts and abilities, roles and relationships. My view is that people's development is social-psychological as well as biogenetic.

Above all, I was able to carry out this study only because these older people took me wholeheartedly into their lives and allowed me to bring their experiences to a wider audience. My special thanks to them.

PATHWAYS TO FAMILY MYTHS

CHAPTER 1

Understanding Family Myths

Sixty-five-year-old Mr. P is constantly worried about his wife's ill health. He describes her as weak and anemic. It is around 6 P.M. Mrs. P leaves the living room to go to the bathroom. Mr. P calls out to his daughter, "Look out for your mother, she might fall." The daughter responds, "Sure dad." Mr. P continues to yell "Your mother is weak. Stay with her as she needs rest and will tire easily." So the daughter runs to the bathroom to help her mother. The daughter is 35 years old, has rarely dated men and has never been married, feeling her mother needed her. Mrs. P is seen as weak and inferior. The daughter plays the role of nurse and helper whenever necessary. The mother enjoys the attention she gets from her daughter and her husband. She holds on to it by being helpless. This helplessness aids in keeping her family together.

Webster's New World Dictionary (College Edition, 1970) describes myth as a traditional story serving to explain some phenomenon or custom. Each myth carries with it a certain theme or motif, as well as our understanding of it.

By understanding cultural myths, we can begin to understand the common needs of people, their relationships, their aspirations and their life-styles. By understanding family myths such

3

as the helplessness of Mrs. P, we can gain important insights into individual and family functioning.

How is a myth defined? The historical definition of a myth includes a story, narration or oral transmission serving usually to explain some phenomenon of nature, the origin of people and institutions, or the customs and religious rites of a people (Ohmann, 1962).

FAMILY MYTHS IN THE LITERATURE

Comparatively few articles have addressed the subject of family myths. The concept of a family myth was initially put forth by Ferreira (1963) and he considered it to be the family's defense mechanism. He called it the pattern of mutually agreed upon, but constricted/rigid roles that family members utilize as a defensive posture. This pattern is not challenged by the family members. Thus, myth reduced the family's flexibility and capacity to respond to new and unrehearsed situations.

Ferreira indicated that the function of family myths is to maintain the homeostasis of the family. It stimulates either healthy or unhealthy family interactions and provides a technique for influencing and managing family members. It serves as a "family engineered canal" through which culture flows from one generation to the next.

In his article, Ferreira (1963) described reality distortions (family myths) in family members' view of each other and the family as a whole. Such distortions are maintained by taboos against discussion of the family myth. Family myths emphasize different themes, such as the myth of happiness or unhappiness in a family, both of which are stereotypes or distortions. Ferreira adds that families seek therapy when the myth is challenged and the equilibrium of the family is upset. The family then wants help merely to return to the previous state of equilibrium.

Byng-Hall (1973) has indicated that family myths can be related directly to life events and painful experiences within the family more readily than any unconscious individual fantasy. An individual's unconscious fantasy may reproduce and articulate the taboo or hidden fear, and hence could be perpetuated by family myths. Family myths provide a bridge that connects life events and unconscious fantasy. Byng-Hall suggests that consensus role images are needed for families to live together. This has important implications for working with families who are extruding one member. To establish a new reality-based consensus may be more urgent a task than to elucidate the nature of a break-up of the old consensus.

Stierlin (1973a) has compared shared fantasies that evolve in small groups. He identifies family myths of harmony, of exculpation and redemption, and of salvation. These myths defend family members against painful confrontations with aspects of their shared history and bar intrusions and unsettling evaluations of the family by the outside world.

Box (1979) illustrated how concepts of myths could be used to help towards understanding and interpreting family groups in therapy. Let me describe her thesis in greater detail as it reveals the family dynamics. The author presented a case of the P family where the function of the family myth was to protect the family from conscious awareness of fear-laden and shared preoccupations; in this particular case it was a preoccupation with the outcome of sexuality. The mythical elements seem to be contained in a message that apart from the two daughters' behavior during the past two years, they were a happy, united and loving family. The mother is shown as a strong, controlling and ruling force in the family compared to a father who emerges as a good, strong-charactered, illness-bound and meek person. The girls' liaisons with sexually exciting but irresponsible boys are seen as the cause of their family problems.

What this myth avoids is the threat of death (the mother is suffering from chronic leukemia) and the fragility and vulnerability existing in the parents' relationship. Box hypothesizes that the feared theme had to do with fantasies about the very damaging and catastrophic outcome of male sexuality and potency. From this perspective, the real threat of death was a dreadful confirmation, rather than a cause, of the fears.

It was to guard against the awareness of this myth that the

parents had adopted their respective defensive positions. The therapist's extreme difficulties in exploring and interpreting, seemed to be a measure of the great anxiety associated with the repudiated theme which was being indirectly expressed by the girls. The losses in function associated with these defensive positions were clearly seen in terms of mother's femininity and receptivity and the father's masculine potency.

The repudiated theme was introduced into the family through the sexual activities of the girls with coarse and uncaring, but exciting, males. It was as though the daughters were relating to a damaging partner, perhaps an image of the damaging father. In the case of Mr. and Mrs. P, sex itself was a casualty produced by damage. In the case of the daughters, the product of sexual activity was the casualty (Box, 1979).

DEFINITION OF FAMILY MYTH

The literature search was only the beginning of my journey. I found that understanding and studying family myths was sometimes astonishing. Family myths can be defined as fairly well-integrated beliefs that are shared by all family members, concerning their role and status in the family. Although these beliefs may represent reality distortions, they are usually unchallenged by the family members. What I assumed to be myths appeared someplace else as folklore or, worse still, superstition. As I discussed, argued and thought through, with my colleagues, I decided to operationalize family myths in a broad fashion that would include different protective and defensive postures in family living. I decided that a family myth could contain folklore, legend, saga, a taboo, a secret or a superstition, a ritual, and/or family rules depending upon what helps the family to stay together irrespective of whether the family myth is negative or positive.

Brunvard (1978) indicates that it is not always possible to establish absolutely whether a given narrative is a myth, a legend or folklore. Folklore as described by Dundes (1965) is orally transmitted, but not all that is orally transmitted is folklore. The term folklore includes such things as folk stories, folk arts, folk medicine, folk belief, and folk custom. The development of any item of folklore is comparable to that of any custom, institution, technique or art form. It is invented at some time by some individual. It can be assumed that many legends or proverbs, like many other cultural inventions, faded away when they became incompatible with newer patterns and traditions. Legends and myths, like folklore, depend on retelling (Brunvard, 1978), just as all aspects of culture are perpetuated by restatement and reenactment.

As this process continues, innovations or modifications are introduced and are adapted gradually to the needs of the society and to the preexisting culture patterns, which may themselves be modified somewhat to conform to the new invention (Dundes, 1965).

Psychoanalysts have made intensive use of the Oedipus story because it represents a splendid example of their general assumption that folklore embodies the substitutive gratifications of desires in people which in the distant past were given free rein but in the course of time were surrendered (Dundes, 1965). These desires are not lost—merely repressed. The repressed desires are to possess the mother and to slay the father. This forms the "Oedipus complex"—a basic tenet of psychoanalytical theory. The story of Oedipus embodies the great psychological reality of the Oedipus complex.

The Oedipus story is viewed by Freud as the expression of an actual historical incident. He postulated that long ago there existed a primal horde, in which an old man retained for himself all the females of the group and drove his sons away from their mothers and sisters. Eventually, the sons got together and killed and ate the old man, after which they committed incest with their mothers and sisters. Later, in remorse for their act of violence toward their father, they tried to atone through a ritual act of commemoration centering around his image, or totem. The feeling of guilt that they felt at that time has been perpetuated through the ages and exists even today in the form of a complex affecting each person in the earlier stages of his lifetime. This complex involves a normal incestuous striving toward the mother and an

ambivalent feeling toward the father, but if these attitudes become fixated, a neurosis develops. From Freud's perspective, it
would not be surprising to find Oedipus-type stories anywhere
in the world as symbolic expressions of the most fundamental
of all human relationships and conflicts (Dundes, 1965).

Legends as described by Boatright, Downs and Flanagan (1958)
are moulded by the narrator and are "here and now" and not
"past" phenomena. Each telling produces a version that is edited
to fit current distortions in family myths. Many secrets involve
information that is either withheld or differentially shared between or among people. The phrase "between or among people" signals that we are squarely in the realm of interpersonal
relationships, and "withheld or differentially shared" immediately suggests the notion of boundaries and alliances, that is, the
structuring of relational systems. Secrets are about real happen-
ings or incidents, such as an extramarital affair, a prison record,
or incest.

Secrets can be classified as individual secrets, internal family
secrets and shared family secrets. An *individual* secret is one that
is kept away from other members of the family. *Internal* family
secrets involve cases in which at least two people keep a secret
from each other. *Shared* family secrets involve cases in which all
members of the family know the secret but are bound to keep
it from each other or persons outside of the family (Karpel, 1980).
For instance, Aunt Emily's drinking may be the family secret and
it would be considered a taboo to discuss it even in front of family
members, not to mention outsiders. The myth that surrounds
this secret indicates that the family is normal and that all aunts
are private people and so is Aunt Emily. Therefore, no one should
"interfere" or intrude into her life-style. This maintains the homeostasis of the family and the secret of the family is well guarded.

Superstitions represent beliefs in the supernatural, in "lucky"
colors and numbers, and in other notions that are inconsistent
with known facts or rational thought. For example, the B family
views Friday the 13th as a day of ill omen and the family as a
whole will not start anything new on this day.

Webster's New World Dictionary (College Edition, 1970) describes taboo as any social prohibition or restriction that results from convention or tradition. Families create their own restrictions about what is acceptable or unacceptable and this would constrict and restrain the behavior of family members accordingly.

Family rules are part of family myth which is transfused and present in the family. Ford (1983) suggests that family rules are seldom explicit and rarely written down. They are implicit; it is the unwritten rule that governs the family. Family rules are also inferences; they are abstractions. Rules may be inferred from any behavior that has occurred often enough for the observer to comment that this behavior had been seen before. Family rules have dimensions of repetition and redundancy. Finally, family rules have autonomy and tend to perpetuate themselves. It is at this level that the rule takes on the qualities of a myth.

Myths explain and prescribe family roles and behavior that are beyond the awareness of its members to a large extent. Myths are present at a meta level and express avoided topics, but these topics are rarely investigated or challenged.

TYPES OF FAMILY MYTHS

1. *The myth of harmony* specifies, "We are all happy," "There are no problems in our family," "We will always be happy" (Stierlin, 1973a).
2. *The myth of the family scapegoat* indicates that all problems are due to one person within the family.
3. *The myth of catastrophism* mentions that all family behavior must conform to certain restrictions in order to avoid catastrophic consequences for family members. If not, a "weak" family member who "cannot take it" will die or become totally helpless.
4. *The myth of pseudomutuality* says that in good families, family members never fight or disagree.
5. *The myth of overgeneralization* views every individual in the family in terms of a restricted set of role expectations. When Tommy is given the restricted role of a "bad kid," it implies that

nothing Tommy does is ever good. Thus, he is pigeonholed into this restricted role and his "badness" is generalized.

6. *The myth of togetherness* suggests that all outsiders are potential enemies and cannot be trusted. Therefore, all family members should stick together regardless of what happens within the family.

7. *The myth of salvation and redemption* looks to some outsider who will come to help the family—a rich uncle, a family therapist, or a new friend (Stierlin, 1973a).

These types of family myths are discussed in greater detail below.

1. Myth of Harmony

This is the family myth that specifies, "We are all happy, there are no problems in our family and we will always be happy." In this myth a beautiful picture is painted of the family's present and past togetherness. However, the harmony is unreal and these families often appear to have conflict-avoidant, psychosomatic problems. Such families have an eagerness and "loving" friendliness with one another that blot out and dissociate past and present disagreements and hostilities. The families utilize their own myths of harmony to cement the dissociation and throw facts into a "memory hole" (Stierlin, 1973a).

A look at the case given below reveals that this message appears to control the behavior of the family members.

In a family of three members—a stepfather, a mother and their child—an illusion was created that everyone was happy. The mother felt grateful that because of her "new husband" she had been spared economic distress and considered her family a happy one, even though both she and her daughter were physically beaten by her husband.

The 15-year-old daughter's position in the family slowly changed; as she grew prettier and more womanly, her stepfather methodically restricted her behavior so that she had no friends and nowhere to go except to school and back. In time they developed an incestuous relationship. At one point the daughter attempted to tell her mother, who hushed her with, "You know, we are a happy family and we have no problems. Paul (stepfather) is sometimes angry with us and this is all because he loves us so much. He would never hurt us."

Paul responded to any accusation about his physical abuse with, "I beat you because I love you. It is comfortable to me to show my anger. I really love you both and we all know that we are a happy family." The wife echoed his thinking, the incest relationship was glossed over, and the daughter remained silent under the burden of incest. She was made to believe that they were a happy family. Thus, in spite of the obvious—and damaging—behavioral patterns, the myth of a happy family with no problems was created.

Such families rewrite the family history as Stalin's and Hitler's textbooks rewrote the history of Russia and Germany (Stierlin, 1973a). In their myths of harmony, family members utilize shared defenses of denial and idealization in their rewriting of history.

2. Myth of the Family Scapegoat

Another family myth is created when family members believe that all problems are caused by a single family member. If this person would "just behave well," everything would be alright.

Thus, one person is singled out as the cause of family problems and is the recipient of family anger. This is the myth of the family scapegoat. People sometimes play the part of the family scapegoat to divert to themselves the evils that threaten others. An ancient Hindu ritual describes how the pangs of thirst could be transferred from one sick person to another. The operator seats the pair on branches, back to back, the sufferer with his face to the East and the healthy man with his face to the West. In this manner he transfers the pangs of thirst from the thirsty soul to the other, who obligingly receives them in his stead (Frazer, 1920).

Among the ancient hunting, pastoral and agricultural peoples there were many customs based on scapegoating. One custom laid the accumulated misfortunes and sins of the people upon a dying god who was supposed to bear them forever, leaving the people innocent and happy. The notion that people can transfer their guilt and sufferings to some other being who will bear the guilt for them is familiar in many primitive societies. It arises from the obvious confusion between the physical and the mental, between the material and the spiritual. Because it is possible to shift a load of wood or stones from one back to another, the primitive man believed that it is equally possible to shift the burden of his pains and sorrows to another, who will suffer them on his behalf (Frazer, 1920).

In classical Rome, every year on the 14th of March a man clad in skins was led in procession through the streets, beaten with long white rods, and driven out of the city. He was called Mamurius Veturius, that is "Old Mars," and the ceremony took place on the day preceding the first full moon of the old Roman year (which began on the first of March). The skinclad man must have represented the Mars of the past year, who was driven out at the beginning of the new one (Frazer, 1920).

The phenomenon of the whipping boy who received the whippings that were supposedly meant to punish the royal prince for his wrongdoings was commonly practiced in Europe, particularly in England. The young boy who was whipped was the scapegoat taking the pain of the young prince's punishment.

Utilizing scapegoats for the benefit of a group of people has been a way of life. Therefore, it is not unusual for families to utilize a single family member as a scapegoat for maintaining the coherence of their family.

In the Smith family, the younger son, Jack, is dyslexic, messy, and considered a troublemaker. Sally, his mother, dumps her anger on him and she is joined by all the other members of the family who collude to single him out as the object of their anger. Sally displaces her anger on Jack who stands for her father and her husband to whom she cannot show anger. The message that Jack constantly hears is, "If it weren't for you, everyone in the family would be happy."

Jack, the scapegoat, responds by acting out the whole family's pain in his disruptive behavior.

3. *Myth of Catastrophism*

Another family myth specifies that behavior must fit certain restrictions in a family. If not, some family member may become helpless or die. Therefore, the family attempts to protect a family member so that the rest of the family may survive. This is the myth of catastrophism.

Fifty-five-year-old John Cain has never been able to hold a job for more than six months. He is not helpful around the house either. He spends most of his time lying around watching TV. However, he is always charming and agreeable with the family. He does not lose his temper with his children and is sympathetic to his wife. His wife, Alice, is overwhelmed by her full-time job and all the household work. The Cain family sees the father as a helpless, weak person. They fear that something terrible might happen to him as it did to his father who had a heart attack while he was shoveling snow. Meanwhile, Alice plays the martyr. The family maintains the process of keeping the father helpless, clumsy and irresponsible with no confrontations. Thus, the behavior of different family members negates family growth.

4. *Myth of Pseudomutuality*

Pseudomutuality refers to the quality of relatedness. The family myth indicates good families never fight or disagree.

There is a myth in the Jackson family that only ''bad people'' fight. The family members constantly say that they are happy. They carry the notion that they belong to a good family and therefore should not fight. This is contradictory to the reality that in a healthy family the emotional climate would allow for feelings of anger to be expressed whenever and wherever appropriate.

Mrs. Jackson is dissatisfied with her life and the financial problems that they face. She did not expect to become the chief supporter of her family. She is not conscious of her anger but views her husband as a burden and spends her time nagging the children and developing constant headaches. Mr. Jackson, who works off and on, spends much of his time drinking. In this family the direct expression of anger is avoided. When the Jackson family talk about themselves outside their household, they describe themselves as a happy family who do not fight at all. ''We talk things over because we have only minor disagreements.''

Wynne et al. (1958) suggest that dysfunctional families, overburdened by their own mythology, often relate to one another by pseudomutuality. The family makes strong efforts to maintain the appearance of a relationship, the illusion that they have an open, mutually understanding way of interacting, while in reality they maintain great distance from one another. What they do seem to have in common is a shared maneuver designed to defend against pervasive feelings of meaninglessness and emptiness among all family members.

In pseudomutual relationships there is anxiety about separating from an established and familiar relationship. Family members together develop the illusion of a perfect fit between their own behavior and expectations and those of each other member. Divergence in viewpoint is intolerable; the illusion of family unity has to be maintained. Any potential for growth or autonomy is sacrificed for the purpose of holding the family together.

To grow up in a pseudomutual setting is to feel part of the self-sufficient social system with its own continuous but unstable family boundaries with the outside world. Wynne describes this type of family boundary as a rubber fence—it stretches to include whatever can be interpreted as complementary to its structure and contracts to exclude that which it considers alien. Thus, the individual family member is prevented from recognizing or taking part in any activity that differentiates that person either within or outside of the family role structure. The surrounding walls expand and contract; one's own perceptions cannot be trusted, and escape is impossible (Wynne, et al., 1958).

5. Myth of Overgeneralization

This family myth prescribes roles to family members. Individual family members are locked into different roles and each individual is seen as a role-maker. Spiegel (1960) describes a role as a goal-directed pattern or sequence of acts tailored by the cultural process for the transactions that a person carries out in a social group or situation, or in a family group. These roles are viewed as having positive or negative values. Each family member takes on a restricted role.

In the Jones family, Mr. Jones does all the housework and holds a full-time job. He is viewed as the ideal parent and husband. Their son, Tom, is the family troublemaker. Mother Jones is viewed as a helpless and weak person incapable of hard work. Daughter Anne is viewed as the helper. This family fixates itself into these different roles, and acts them out repeatedly. Tom is not kind or caring, because he has to play the role of the troublemaker to satisfy the needs of this family. In a similar manner, if the daughter wishes to be negative she has no permission to show any divergence in viewpoint, interest, role or attitude as this could lead to disruption of family relationships, which is forbidden. A strong sense of personal identity, which requires testing out of different roles and getting honest and meaningful feedback information from others in order to develop, is achieved only with difficulty. Any efforts to assert such individuality are likely to be perceived as a threat to the family. (Goldenberg and Goldenberg, 1980)

6. Myth of Togetherness

This myth requires that families stay together irrespective of their problems.

The Brown family members utilize evasions, denials, placating, and direct lying to work out their problems. There is no family permission for individual members to follow their own unique sense of style, taste, timing, and space. The central theme of such families is to follow certain prescribed personality patterns. Thus, everyone in the family is musical/fat/messy/outgoing, etc. and they will always stand by one another. In such families, injunctions are so strong that members obey them for life. Whatever is done for the family as a whole is important and any other behavior is minimized. Incest is a classic example of families staying together irrespective of their problems.

When 50-year-old John Brown has an incestuous relationship with his daughter, it is viewed as a family secret. The myth prevails that the family should stay together regardless of this problem. This theme is constantly highlighted in the family and the incest relationship is overlooked.

7. Myth of Salvation and Redemption

At times a family myth is created which specifies that an outsider will enter the family and "save" it. This could be a rich uncle who would leave the family a large fortune, or a new family member, or a grandparent, or a family therapist. Once this outsider enters the family through money or person, the family believes that all their problems will be solved and they will live happily ever after—an outcome that cannot happen if the myth is to survive. This is the myth of salvation which provides the family with a shared belief that the pain, injustice and suffering inherent in family life can somehow be avoided or undone through the meaningful intervention of some strong, if not omnipotent, figure or agency. This myth distorts facts, concerning the family members' real past and present involvements with each other (Stierlin, 1973a).

Forty-year-old Jane had been withdrawn and constantly depressed. Her family background appeared to be chaotic. Her father had deserted the family and had a lover. He died suddenly at his lover's house. The family was devastated. The death of the father, combined with the circumstances under which it happened, affected all the members of the household. Jane stopped eating, could not sleep, and would not speak to anyone.

Jane's family consisted of the mother, three brothers and a sister. The mother visited a therapist and told her at the first interview "We want you to make Jane alright, then she will be happy and we will all be alright." The fact that Jane was 40 years of age, had never held a job, and had been dependent upon her mother for everything was overlooked. The illusion that the therapist could "save" Jane and, through her, the rest of the family was firmly implanted in the family's thinking.

To deal with this situation the cooperation of all family members is required and this includes the victim delegate. The victim delegate may win or lose. By allowing himself or herself to be victimized, this person may "enjoy" psychological power over others (Boszormenyi-Nagy and Spark, 1973).

In the Benson family, children were not allowed to talk about their natural mother, Rita, who had been described to them as a "bad, evil, irresponsible and corrupt" person. The story said that she had run away with a useless drunkard after being married to Mr. Benson for 10 years and having mothered four children. She was the deserter and the family had to dislike and blame her for their problems.

Naturally, there was a great amount of pain and depression in the family. The children's new stepmother, who was barely out of her teens, was considered to be the savior of the family, and was viewed as the "model mother," even though she felt burdened and overwhelmed by her responsibilities. The Bensons were also aware that the father had hardly participated in any family activities and had been in and out of love with many women. This was overlooked because this family jointly projected their anger onto the natural mother, who was an absentee. The new mother was viewed as the martyr who would "save the family."

Family myths give us patterns of personal behavior that help us at each stage in our lives. For instance, modern myth heroes help children through inevitable fears arising from their smallness and dependency. Superman and Superwoman feed children's natural fantasies of being strong, fantasies that keep them from being overwhelmed by a world of large and mysteriously powerful adults.

Family myths have an effect on individual behavior and this will be seen as we view the different cases; family myths protect and defend the family and thus perform a validating or justifying function that maintains the coherence of the family.

FAMILY MYTHS AS SACRED AND TABOO

In some families there are a few "secret" emotional themes. Unpleasant topics are not discussed. Families constantly move towards keeping themselves "worry free." But there are constant fears, many times unfounded, about taboo topics being discussed. Taboo topics could be the result of long-standing multigenerational conflicts or could relate to current problems. An emotional climate is regulated in the family where each family member contributes to the happiness or unhappiness in the family with compliance to retain the family coherence. Behavior may be accepted, overlooked, or endorsed because of the loyalty family members feel toward each other.

A loyal member of a family internalizes the spirit and expectations of the family. He or she also develops a set of specific attitudes to comply with the internalized injunctions. Failure to comply with family obligations would lead to guilt feelings and social pressures among family members. Thus, there are layers of loyalty in families.

This issue of loyalty is closely related to alignments, splits, alliances and subgroup formations (Boszormenyi-Nagy and Spark, 1973). Loyalty commitments are invisible but held together by strong threads that blend complex pieces of relationship behavior in families as well as in larger society. In order to understand the functions of a group of people, we need to know who are bound together in loyalty and what loyalty really means to them. It appears that every person maintains an account of what has been invested in the system and what has been withdrawn in the form of support received or one's exploitative use of others. These are invisible accounts of obligations.

In families the fundamental loyalty commitment is to the maintenance of the group itself. Boszormenyi-Nagy and Spark (1973) indicate that people have to go beyond conscious behavioral manifestations and specific issues if they want to understand the meaning of basic loyalty commitments. What appears to be shockingly destructive and irritating behavior on the part of one member towards another may not be experienced as such by those involved as this conforms to a basic family loyalty.

> Fifty-five-year-old Uncle Dick was the family ghost because he was mentally retarded. The family did not accept the mental retardation nor did they discuss or offer him special treatment. He was treated like other family members and if he needed help with reference to any bodily function or with money, family members would constantly say, "Well, he's a little slow today." Of course, he was slow every day. His need for special training was overlooked. Though Uncle Dick's nephews and nieces had become educated, sophisticated adults, the myth that their uncle was normal was perpetuated by all family members and went unchallenged though this was a distinct distortion of reality. The retardation was a secret and a taboo topic both within the family and in discussions with outsiders.

Many times, family taboos are false and mirage-like, but they are accepted in the family by everyone as something that no one dares to investigate or challenge. One of the members in Dick's family who was a psychologist was aware that the uncle was mentally retarded, but did not acknowledge it.

When a large number of taboos and secrets rule a household, the family members are likely to be dysfunctional to some degree and suffer from low self-esteem. They probably have not differentiated themselves as individuals in the family. They may solidify a relationship where the boundaries between self and other become blurred. In this situation, the uniqueness of self is acknowledged only covertly, if at all. There is an expectation of family loyalty even if it smothers family members.

In the Clark family, Friday was considered to be an unlucky day. Everybody simply accepted this superstition without discussing it; they were not really aware of the taboo. Grandmother Clark had died on this day years ago but her death was not discussed in the family. Death was a taboo topic and family members only whispered about it. Contrary to the belief that she had died that fateful Friday, she had actually been murdered by her husband when he found her with her lover; thus she was killed in a family "fight." There was no family permission for any member to discuss this topic; they simply followed the family rules that said that nothing good could be done on that day and all family members were brainwashed into thinking that this particular day was unlucky.

Loyalty to the family was firmly ingrained in all the family members. There was boundary setting about what family members could discuss and the topic of death was shrouded in fear, anger and silence. The family boundaries allowed this family to live with its own taboos and secrets and retain its coherence.

In families where there is little differentiation among family members, the desire to hold the family together is much more important than dealing with reality.

In some families, assumptions are made about different family members: "Peter is strong," "Kim is noisy," "Jack is sick." Family members are pigeonholed and labeled. Singling out and scapegoating a particular family member as the cause of family problems, as well as recipient of family anger, is common.

FAMILY MYTHS AS COMPROMISE AND DEFENSE

A family myth represents the way in which the family appears to its members and is a part of the inner image of the group, an image which all family members contribute to and attempt to preserve. The family myth refers to identified roles that family members take on individually or collectively, subconsciously or consciously, for the sake of the family.

> In the Richardson family it was expected that all women would be brave and stand up for themselves. This was due to an incident in the family history.
>
> Mary Richardson had grown up in a small town in West Virginia where she lived with her grandfather. He was the head teller of a bank in this small town and they lived in a brick house right next to the bank.
>
> One night—around the year 1885—she heard a noise and looked out of the window. She could see some men trying to break into the bank. She woke up her grandfather, which was a gutsy thing to do, considering he was like a bear. He took his horse pistol out of the bedside table, pointed it out of the window, and fired at the bandits, who ran away. He didn't hit any of them.
>
> The bank, in gratitude, gave Mary a Smith and Wesson .32 pearl-handled special. She used to take it out into the country in the fall—this is how she tells it—and she'd stand on a bridge. As the leaves blew off the trees, she'd go bang! bang! She claimed to be a good shot.
>
> Sometime afterwards, she was again awakened by a noise in the bank next door. This time she skipped her grandfather, the middleman, and just leaned out the window herself with her gun blazing away. Like roota-toot-toot! It's the bandits!
>
> This gang got caught at the ferry trying to cross the Shenandoah river. And according to her story, at the trial—when they were tried and sentenced to 25 years in jail or whatever—they said, "If it hadn't been for that damn little girl, we would have gotten away clean." (Zeitlin, Kotlin and Baker, 1982)

The myth in the Richardson family said that women were capable of taking care of themselves and others and were always brave—everyone of them! In this home, the word "fear" was a taboo.

> Sixty-year-old Peter represented his family myth in terms of being a womanizer just like all the other men in his family.

His family myth established that he was "weak" towards
women, because he couldn't help it. He lived up to it. He
had been married three times and fooled around sufficiently
to lose all his wives and his children.

The concept of living up to the family's expectations is a powerful bind into which family members could be placed.

In the Edwards family the mother was always smiling, irrespective of what problems were present in the family. She
was considered to be the "happy one." Even when she was
in great pain, she had a frozen plastic smile. However,
everyone walked around in her home accepting that nothing
really bothered her even though she had a daughter who
was acting out in high school and a husband who was a
heavy drinker with a history of holding jobs for only short
periods of time.

   She was greatly admired by her husband and children for
her "sensitivity" and her ability to keep cool. She knew her
husband had a lover, but there was no apparent sadness—
instead she smiled. . . . She was 48 years of age and had
developed a permanent smile. None of her children did well
with their lives and her only son wound up like her husband with a bad work record and alcoholism. But all the
children crowded around "mama" because she was always
cheerful and smiled.

In this family, the family myth represents an agreed-upon level
of compromise in which every family member obtained some satisfaction.

   A family myth serves the function of protecting and defending
the family. It is supported by all family members and the family
is able to resist any outside attempt to shake or challenge the accepted group image. At times, individual members may be aware
of the fantasy nature of some aspect of the family's inner image,
but they are quick to adopt a preassigned role and block out the
awareness they might otherwise possess.

   The family myth modifies the cognitive context of family behavior and it provides ready-made explanations of family norms.

Family myths have an economic value as well and often they are necessary for the legitimization and consecration of an ongoing relationship. It might appear that family myths are played out by different members, but the purpose or motive involves the whole system of relationships. Negative behavioral patterns such as compulsions, obsessions, hysterical attacks, suicidal gestures, and delinquency are part of the family myth (Ferreira, 1963).

Through a family collusion, the family members create an unspoken agreement that maintains the family's stability. This can help in the growth of individual members and promote family growth or it can negate individual and family growth. Those negative collusions which are really in defense of the family's coherence are scapegoating, hidden agendas, and assumption-making. There are hidden subjects and information that keep the family in conflict. In some families there is assumption-making that indicates that a family member knows the facts, feelings, and motivations that involve other family members and what makes them function. Family alliances, which are subgroups banding together for protection and power, are common phenomena. Positive myth-making assumptions such as, "George is a genius," "Kathy will make it to the top," "We are all winners," and so on place positive pressures on families as family members attempt to live up to the myths.

When family myths are used as defenses, the most important compromise that the family makes is to view the problem as residing in one person. Many times it could be a child—the most vulnerable—who is the designated patient or client. The identified person may be described as being highly troublesome, but the idea of family myths implies the use of role and role images to hide more disturbing conflicts. Families might also use restrictive family defenses in their functioning if they find that alternatives could be catastrophic and no new models are available.

Adult and young members at times compromise their behaviors and potentials to fit a family system. This compromise appears in the form of family myths—a child becoming sick for a long period of time or a family that rotates around the unemployment of a parent. These are compromises that family members create and function from; the family myth serves as a form of defense against facing reality as it is. Disturbed families have an amazing capacity to induce collusive denial systems in the family. Different family members rotate around roles that are specifically required by the family. For this purpose, family myths do add form and content to the family.

A CONCEPTUAL FRAMEWORK FOR FAMILY MYTHS

I believe that family myths are formed to help the family system maintain itself without making any major changes. They restrict family experiences by curbing certain feelings and transactions that could take place in a family.

How could we view family myths in a way that would be useful in understanding styles of behavior in the family? We could describe ourselves as omnipotential beings in the sense that we choose and concentrate on certain potentials that become part of our personality and at the same time deny parts of our self that may be unsafe to accept. Thus, restriction of behavior in oneself could become acceptable behavior to others.

Developmentally, myths may be classified as *couples'* myths, *cross-generational* myths and *disjointed* myths.

The Couples' Myth

This myth develops with shared denials of reality. The first form of collusion in a couple thus gets established in marriage, with *denial* as a similar split for these two individuals. This denial of self begins in their own families of origin where each person, for instance, is told and later learns not to show anger. As this is not allowed in the family, it becomes the denied part of self and is brought into the marriage. This couple forms what is called a "joint false self" and a brittle defense that indicates, that showing anger, for example, is not good. Through rules of interaction and norms of the family, the children enter into a coalition with the parents as an aid to each other's denial. In this family, the family myth, "Don't show your anger," is developed.

The second form of collusion takes place when one is matched with an individual who by nature has developed different potentials. At first, one is attracted by what one is "unable to do." As Dicks (1967) indicates, this could be based on an attraction to a marital partner who is viewed unconsciously as a symbol of the "lost" or repressed aspects of a subject's personality. These two people may get married to each other because of opposite traits. Thus, each partner finds the split-off aspects of his or her personality in the other partner—for example, an aggressive husband and a submissive wife. But in a more hidden form there is the wife's repressed aggression and the husband's denied submissiveness, which could appear at times in overt behavior. Usually this aspect of the marriage is hidden by sexual urgency and idealization of courtship and early marriage.

When the partner is confronted solidly by the denied part of himself or herself present in the other person, there is a potential for using it either in a constructive manner in mending internal splits or for establishing a collusive defense. In this latter situation, each partner attempts to disown the unacceptable aspects of his or her self when they show up in the other person, thus helping to maintain one's own defenses. This could lead to "dog and cat" (incompatible) marriages that can neither be mended nor broken up (Byng-Hall, 1973).

Skynner (1969) indicates that families utilize projection, splitting and denial as part of the family myths to protect the family.

According to Byng-Hall (1973), there are three patterns of images that are relevant in maintaining a family myth: (1) ideal self-images, the behavior towards which each person strives or pressures others to follow or adapt; (2) the consensus role images—by common consent, the family agrees on the roles that each family member should play. When individuals are away from the family group, they may admit having secret reservations about the validity of these images, but they revert to this type when they visit home; (3) repudiated images—family members might be specific about these but they can only be inferred from the rising anxiety or the diversionary techniques that occur when certain topics are raised or sequences of interaction are initiated. The degree and extent of vehemence or disgust with which the roles are denied or attributed to someone else can convey the quality of the repudiation. In other families, observable, often nonverbal patterns of transactions occur of which the family is not aware.

The Cross-Generational Myth

The ideal self-images, the consensus role images and the repudiated images are relevant to family myths and are recruited in cross-generational myths, couple and disjointed myths. Cross-generational myths arise when the parents' marriage is based on mutual idealization, producing a "joint false self." Children may be linked to the marital collusion by processes of secondary identification and projective identification (Byng-Hall, 1973). The adolescents may be required to conform to parental self-images by not damaging the basic integrity of the parental "good" internal objects that are being reinforced by identification with "good" children. The reciprocal process of children identifying with parents is, of course, a part of normal development, but it could play a part in the mechanism of mutual idealization. At times, children are recruited as an aid to each other's denial. Through a collusive marital system, children are incorporated to maintain the parents defense systems. Those marriages that are defending against unresolved child-parent difficulties are likely to recruit children into major roles in the defensive system.

Many times, marital defenses are created around factors like genital sexuality or violence. There was an older woman who came from a moralistic home and married a man who was alcoholic and beat and abused her. She repeatedly told her three daughters that "men were bad and sex was repulsive." As the children grew older they learned to dislike men and sex. It did create maturational problems for the children in the family, and one daughter had been in therapy for a long time.

The family consensus image could lead to impoverished family life, with family myths that give similar roles to all family members. "We are a happy/intellectual/quiet family." If this is based on a capacity to enjoy life and also deal with angry or conflictual situations, then it is not a family myth. However, if a family cannot tolerate ambivalence, denies the consensus script, and hides the opposite feared or taboo drama, then it becomes a family myth that is too carefully followed by family members (Byng-Hall, 1973).

The Disjointed Myth

Disjointed family myths appear when there are unresolved crises in a family like a failed mourning or a desertion or a sudden death of a younger person; the image of the lost person becomes resurrected in a remaining member of the family.

Family myths also develop due to loyalty to the family where denial and avoidance and fear are often fairly significant ingredients.

UNIVERSALITY OF FAMILY MYTHS

Family myths are a universal phenomenon, not the exclusive property of families with problems. Most families have myths that can be either positive or negative. I remember a legendary family therapist I met when I was struggling to understand what family myth really meant. This great, big, tall man looked at me and said that he was a family myth. His parents expected him to perform and he had performed. He studied, wrote, developed new concepts and practiced family therapy. He added with a smile that he had, in fact, performed for the next three generations as well. He smiled contentedly as he continued, "I realized a few years ago that I was the positive family myth."

Family myths may be the result of reciprocal role relationships that have been developed between husbands, wives and children.

Based on the needs of a particular family group, myths become intertwined in different family systems. Some myths are positive and help towards the growth of a family and others are negative and retard the growth of a family. All family myths protect and defend the family system.

METHODOLOGY OF THE STUDY

The present research study was conducted at an institutional setting for elderly people.

According to the latest statistics, about 85 percent of the elderly live in their own homes or with their children. My hypothesis is that residents of a county home as a group are poorer, more sick physically, and have less adequate support systems than those who live in the community. This institutionalized group of elderly people was purposely chosen to find out if family myths persist in the life of an individual even when this person lives away from his or her family and its support systems. What are the types of family myths that evolved in their own families? How powerful are families and to what degree do they exert their control? These were some of the initial questions I had in mind when I started to develop this study.

In the institution studied, there were 700 elderly people. Out of this number, 73 were chosen by the administrator and his assistants in various units as people who were alert and could be interviewed. Thirty members were chosen randomly. Five members refused to participate.

Semistructured interviewing was the primary tool by which information was obtained. Each elderly person was interviewed for about three to four hours. All interviews were audiotaped. Adequate time was allowed for unstructured conversation. This proved to be helpful in obtaining additional information as well as giving the elderly people an opportunity to ventilate and reminisce.

The age group of the elderly studied, ranged from over 65 to one person who was 91 years of age. Fourteen women and 11 men were studied.

In the sample of 25 people, two were born outside of the United States. All of the interviewees were blue collar workers or women married to blue collar workers. Out of the 25 interviewees, two (one man and one woman) were married, two men were divorced, three men had never married, and the rest were widowed. None of the interviewees had a college education and most belonged to the Catholic church and practiced their religion.

We tried to cover the life sequence that included the family of origin, marriages, and the family of procreation. Questions included notions about marriage and relationship with spouse(s), children, and in-laws. (Appendix 1 reproduces the semistructured interview). As the interviews progressed, incidents began to unfold in a particular sequence. Often, the interviews became time-consuming but they proved to be beneficial for the elderly persons who got a chance to tell their story in their own fashion. The interviewer had to intervene a number of times to get the story straight, to learn about specific situations, positive or negative, and the feelings that went with them. Many important life events and crisis points that had not been resolved also began to appear. Although this was not a therapeutic interview, there may have been some therapeutic effects. Most of the interviewees viewed this as a worthwhile undertaking.

The primary aim was to discover family myths among this group of elderly men and women.

Four subjects were chosen and interviewed at least five times for a total of 12 to 15 hours in three and a half months. Among the four were two men, one currently married and one divorced, and two women, one currently married and one a widow. This gave an overall picture of the elderly as we tried to maximize the diversity of the group in terms of background and life courses. Here the case study approach was utilized to attain a deeper understanding of their family life-styles and thereby discover the presence of family myths.

On many occasions I immersed myself in the interview material and worked towards an intuitive understanding of the interviewees and the presence of myths in their lives. Slowly I tried more interpretive formulations and, going back and forth between the interviews and the analysis, came to a construction of the life course of each of these four people and the presence of family myths in their life course. I utilized the phenomenological analysis when I attempted to ascertain the perceptual framework of the elderly. In phenomenological theory, the perception and experience of the person or subject are always important for they make it possible for the researcher to predict behavior and explain the theory (Crandall, 1980).

These four people represented different life-styles. The spouses of the married interviewees were also interviewed. These people were not representative of any occupational group. Each was special in different ways and had his/her own kind of uniqueness.

The four subjects were interviewed by me. The interviewing of the other 21 interviewees was shared by the two-member research team. In choosing the four cases, I did not choose one over another because he or she was interesting, dull, neurotic or well adjusted. The criteria of choosing these people was based, first, on their ability to be verbal. Secondly, they were chosen for variety, rather than representativeness—a widow, a divorced man, and two married people. I shall briefly introduce them here.

Emily Crosby (all names are fictitious) was 80 years of age, tall, buxom, and fair with blue eyes and silver hair, almost regal looking. Both her husbands were dead. Her first husband had worked on the railroad and her second husband had owned a small store. She had mothered two children.

Paul Fink was 70 years of age and had been married three times. He was living with his third wife at the agency. He was silver-haired and blue-eyed with a hoarse low voice that would easily disappear in a soft murmur. He had worked as an interior decorator and his room revealed his artistic taste in paintings and wall decorations. He was confined to a wheelchair since part of one leg had been frostbitten. His nose was permanently bloated and disfigured due to damage to his body in a snowstorm.

Melissa Simpson was 72 years of age. She was petite and pretty, with soft features that easily crinkled into a pleasant smile. She had brown eyes and silver hair. She had been married two times. Her first marriage lasted for a period of 42 years. Her second husband lived with her at this agency. Her first husband had worked in a factory and her second husband had owned his own business. They moved into the agency three years previously because of ill health; she and her husband had heart problems.

Seventy-two-year-old John Howard was a tall dark man with silver hair and deep-set brown eyes. He had worked as a salesman. He had a pleasant face that broke into a smile easily. He was confined to a wheelchair because of problems in a leg. He was divorced and had been living with his lady friend till he came to this agency two years ago.

The lives of these four people will be studied and presented in four different chapters. In the course of this journey, family behaviors unfold and myths that are hidden in the interrelationships of people will reveal themselves as we tread the intricate routes of joy and pain that these members experienced.

CHAPTER 2

Family Myths and Family Relationships

In this chapter, the 25 people who were studied will be presented in terms of marriage myths, family myths, and myths regarding relationships with children and in-laws. I recognize that 25 people are an unrepresentative sample drawn from an unrepresentative population. Though I quantify my findings, I will concentrate on the most common themes that emerged from the interviews.

MARRIAGE MYTHS AND MARRIAGE DANCES

Every couple that marries performs its own marriage dance. Marriage begins like a dance where through repetition of action the partners obtain grace and ease. Marriage norms are developed through repeated coordinated thinking and action that create their own philosophy for a family.

When a marriage takes place, one myth that is almost always present is the belief that people marry because they love each other. However, reasons for marriage are varied. People may marry because they are lonely. The assumption is that a partner would help to overcome their boredom and restlessness. Such marriages take place because a person is desperate. At times, marriage is viewed as a way of bettering a person's economic future; women often marry for the purpose of feeling financially secure. Others marry because they unconsciously wish to improve themselves. At times the initial attraction is to a person whose qualities the person desires: an inherent liar is attracted to a naive person, an alcoholic to a nondrinker, and so forth. However, spouses learn that intimacy does not bring about self-improvement. Marital partners in time learn to blame each other and marital discord begins (Lederer and Jackson, 1968).

At times, the motivation for a marriage appears to be self-abuse. There are individuals who enjoy suffering and may unconsciously choose partners with whom they can fight, abuse, or degrade themselves. As one man told his wife, "I beat you because I love you," and such behavior is sometimes called the expression of love.

Others marry because they are on the lookout for a parental figure and choose partners who would apparently play that role in their lives.

Lederer and Jackson (1968) indicated that in many workable marriages both spouses got a good deal of mileage out of fantasy. They found that love was often an excuse for domination or control.

I found that people usually had some idea of what their expectations were from marriage. Most of the women interviewees came out with the response, "I wanted a good husband," and both men and women came out with, "I wanted to raise a family," and "I wanted to share my life with another person."

Some viewed marriage as a cure-all for their problems, thinking that problems would be easily resolved if they shared their life with a partner as this would mean two people against the world. Some people viewed marriage as a mythical solution to life's problems.

Seventy-five-year-old Charlotte with her plain looks mentioned that she had eloped with her boyfriend whom she viewed as her rescuer from the negative, unhappy, and lonely situation in her home. Somehow she felt that marriage would cure her unhappiness and loneliness. With a trace of bitterness she discussed her own marriage dance. She was 17 and did all the work in her mother's house. When 27-year-old John came along, she viewed him as her escape from the drudgery of housework and loneliness. Brushing an imaginary hair from her forehead, she added that she wonders now why she thought marriage was a cure for housework. She found after her first bloom of happiness that their romantic love was over. Marriage carried with it the same obligations as being a member of any household except that in a marriage it was your own home and your problems and pleasures.

At the time of her marriage she could not bear to be separated from her husband even for a few hours, but the honeymoon was over all too quickly. He was abusive and a drunkard. He tortured and beat her. She was terrified of him and soon returned to her mother's house, but he forcibly took her back. After living with him for six more months, she ran away, not to her parents' house but off on her own. She never saw her husband again.

Charlotte gave birth to a baby and brought up the child by herself. Gruffly, she added, "I learnt my lesson." To the question whether she had ever thought of remarrying she responded that once was enough, all men were bad, they could not be trusted—a generalization that came out of her own painful experience. There was a kind of abruptness, coldness and crudity in her that constantly and silently screamed at the interviewer, "Shut up and leave me alone." Apologetically, I dared to intrude again. "How's your daughter?" "She's happy. She never married," she answered, as if marriage was always bad. Thus, her early marital cure-all myth appeared to have shattered with the dying of the romantic love that existed between the couple.

Marriage and Love

Often, in a new relationship, a number of assumptions are made about love. I believe it is extremely difficult to retain the first flush of romance in a long-term relationship. Lederer and Jackson (1968) specify that during courtship a number of individuals lose most of their ability to make judgments. They describe courtship as the time of ecstatic paralysis and this is cleverly designed by nature to draw members into reproducing themselves. During the period of courtship, a man and woman are often in a kind of trance, and by the magic of nature they become wonderfully attractive to each other.

Most people believe that they are marrying for love. Though couples may feel romantic during their engagement or early marriage period, romantic love is different from mature love. In romantic love, separation from the partner causes pain; the need to be close to each other is intense. Romantic love has a tinge of selfishness to it. Often the lover is sorry for himself or herself, grieves over his or her loss of pleasure and intimacy, and often has pangs of jealousy. Romantic love is exciting but it is not the same as mature love. Sullivan (1965) indicates that when the satisfaction or security of another person becomes as significant as one's own satisfaction or security, then the state of love exists.

Another family myth indicates that most married people love each other. However, in this study it was seen that none of the older people spoke in terms of love. If this was the underlining to their relationship, it was not specified. They spoke in terms that described their spouse as follows: "Jack is a good provider," "Jill is a good mother to the children," and so forth.

In marriages characterized by poor relationships, each spouse who was interviewed said, and believed tenaciously, that he or she was the "better and more caring" partner.

> In speaking of her marriage, Katherine described herself as "the good person" and her husband as "not such a good provider." He used to bring home friends and inform his wife that he would teach her to be sociable. In fact, his sociability was exaggerated. He talked too much and put her down. By the time their friends had left, loudly and noisily, Katherine felt that she was a lousy cook and housekeeper, a wallflower, helpless and useless. She viewed his behavior as nagging and as an attempt to make her feel helpless and incompetent. But she added with dignity as she raised herself in her seat, "We did not believe in divorce, because

we are good Christians." Thus they lived their lives. He persuaded her that she could never equal him and thereby satisfy him, but he believed that he was always helpful. There was resentment in Katherine's voice and in a martyred tone she added, "We lived our lives together irrespective of any problem, not like these days when people break up so easily. We were more enduring and better."

Marriages where behavior appears to be loving or caring are sometimes characterized by a form of one-upmanship and lack of consideration. Deception of oneself and others is destructive whether or not it leads to the actual disintegration of the marriage. Often the dreamed-of happy marriage does not really materialize. There are negatives and positives in each partner that may accelerate misunderstandings and bickerings. Frustration, confusion, belligerence, and disappointment are part of the spousal relationship (Lederer and Jackson, 1968).

Another myth that people carry around is that they would be married happily ever after. Among the men who were interviewed, seven out of eight (88 percent) said that they were happily married. Some said that they were happy because of their children. One man described his wife as a good person. Another said his home life was happy because he had to spend a lot of time outside of home moonlighting on an extra job because the money he brought home was never sufficient. However, he had a happy marriage. His wife never complained about his being away from home.

One man asked, "What do you expect me to say? We would like people to think that we had a happy marriage because it is a shame to say otherwise, particularly when she is dead." This suggests that loyalty to the partner or the family is also a factor in the responses that were made. The concept of loyalty is both a group characteristic and a personal attitude. As Boszormenyi-Nagy and Spark (1973) put it, the frame of reference is trust, merit, commitment and action; the ethical obligation component in loyalty is first tied to the arousal in the loyalty-bound members of the family of the sense of duty, fairness and justice. Any failure to comply with obligations leads to guilt feelings, which then constitute a secondary regulatory system. With reference to this particular question, loyalty commitments appeared to be closely intertwined with the notion of myths, which function like invisible but strong fibers holding together complex pieces of relationship behavior in families.

Apparently this was not true in Tony's case.

> Tony felt that he had not had a happy marriage. He was divorced and felt that life had cheated him. Based on his own description of his marriage, there were too many disparities. At times, an individual in a marriage may be egocentric and behave like someone who is not married. Tony continued to behave like a bachelor even after his marriage. His wife did not approve and left him. He described his marriage in the following manner: "Separately we were nice people, but together we were terrible."

Among the women, 11 out of 14 (78 percent) mentioned that they were happily married, as suggested by such responses as: "He was a nice man," "We were good to each other," "He was kind to me," "I was a happy girl," "I loved life and he was part of my life." One woman said she was happy that she was separated from her husband because he was "a bad person." This woman described herself as inexperienced when she got married. In such situations, the question of who dominates over the relationship is understood within the parameters of power. It appeared that the husband had dominated the marriage completely. Thus, with the seesaw tilting towards the husband's side, the wife felt that she lost out in the marriage. She continued to be resentful towards her husband even after five decades.

Responses concerning mental happiness seemed to be a function of how the marriage had ended. If a couple had remained married until one of them died, there appeared to be a feeling of loyalty to that person and a desire to say that they had been happily married. But if the marriage was broken by divorce or desertion, there seemed to be no need to say anything positive about the spouse or the marriage.

The Togetherness Myth

Often, the notion of a romantic marriage dwells on complete symbiosis or togetherness. In actuality, the development of some autonomy is inevitable and obviously desirable under most circumstances—but some forms are more acceptable to a particular husband and wife than others.

Usually, young people get the message that a perfect marriage is one in which there is a large degree of togetherness. How possible is it to maintain a relationship with complete togetherness? The romantic-romantic partners fit together like two pieces of a jigsaw puzzle, two parts that are incomplete by themselves but together constitute a whole (Sager, 1976). In a romantic relationship there is passion, openness, intimacy, and pervasive interdependence, but it tends to run downhill within a few years. Because the diminution of intensity is regarded as a loss of love, many couples are not able to make the transition to a satisfactory long-term bond.

The change in intensity rarely occurs simultaneously in both partners. The one who still needs the intense togetherness often reacts strongly to changes in the partner's subtle and overt behavior. These changes usually arouse guilt, a sense of being fenced in, or a desire to withdraw from an intimacy that is regarded as controlling or engulfing by the partner who now wants a different kind of relationship, one based more on companionship and sharing than on the previous level of intensity. This can be devastating to the other partner who experiences the change as a loss of security and love. It may lead to the establishment of a new romantic-romantic relationship with someone else in order to experience again the intense high of being in love (Sager, 1976).

To the question about doing things together, five out of eight (62 percent) of the men who had been married felt that couples should have some separate activities with each partner's knowledge and permission. Three men (38 percent) felt that a married couple should do things together because this is what marriage is all about. Among the married women, 11 (78 percent) felt that they should do things together, though in actuality this did not happen. One woman mentioned that going to church was the only thing they did together. Another mentioned that she enjoyed visiting relatives and even though her husband did not like it he always went along with her. Three women (22 percent) mentioned that they had not done things with their husbands, because their marriages were unhappy and they did not have any common interests.

Marriage as a Problem-Solver

Did these people believe that once they were married all their problems would be solved? In this idea was enmeshed the myth of a perfect marriage. Among the men, four out of eight (50 percent) felt that all problems were solved when they got married. The problems varied from loneliness to physical complaints that disappeared when they had someone to share their lives. Three (37 percent) felt that marriage was not a solution to their problems though companionship with a woman helped. Some of them mentioned financial problems as the reason for differences. More men mentioned that their wives had it easy! All they had to do was stay home, take care of the children and cook meals; it was the man who was the breadwinner, who had to go out and make money and take care of the family's needs. At times this created problems, particularly when the money was not sufficient.

Among the women, nine out of 14 (64 percent) felt that their problems were solved once they had a home of their own. One woman mentioned that her husband was a good man and he took good care of her. She did not have to deal with any problems: "I was a good girl and I did not give him any trouble after marriage and we had a good marriage." This seems to resemble the parental partner combination that Sager (1976) describes in which the parental partner finds a complementary person who will interact as a child. Thus, this interaction elicits the complementary profile from the other. When neither partner is ambivalent about his or her spouse's role, the two tend to do quite well. Many good combinations developed in this manner. However, if life circumstances such as illness or unemployment affect the parental partner, this would cause a change in roles and a tremendous stress on the relationship. The parent-partner may feel threatened or degraded or burdensome. Or the child-partner may become unable to assume responsibilities. The marriage solves problems to the extent that the individual needs of the couple are met in this situation.

Secrets in Marriage

Do husbands and wives have secrets from each other? People felt that in a good marriage a spouse did not hold secrets for it would not help to sustain a marriage. Seven men (86 percent) mentioned that they did not have secrets from their wives; however, when asked to elaborate, some of them said that they did have "innocent" secrets but would not really elaborate on them. It appeared as if the myth of a perfect marriage might be shattered by confessing that they had secrets since secrets were connected with a bad marriage. The respondents did not wish to fall into that category. One person admitted to keeping secrets from the spouse.

> Good-looking Christopher had been separated from his wife for a long period of time; he admitted that he had not confided in her. To him, she was a naive woman who had to be protected and taken care of. She did not know anything about life and he had to teach her even "basic things." When questioned on what these things were, he smiled and said things that young women do not know about. He tried to teach her adult ways but it appeared as if she would never learn. At first he enjoyed her dependency and her constant need for him and his approval. Eventually, this made him uneasy and anxious, particularly after they had a child. He wanted someone to respond to his own needs. He was tired of being the permanent nurturer, so he started going out with other women.

Among the women, nine (64 percent) felt that they did not have secrets from their husbands. One woman came out with this response: "We were good people, why should we have secrets?"

Another interesting answer was: "We had true love in our marriage and therefore had no secrets." Still another person came out with: "Only if you are bad you have secrets and we were good people." It appeared as if they had to deny any secrets because this would mean that they were not loyal to their men. One woman said that she did not have any secrets from her husband because if she did not tell him everything he would beat her. However, he was a good provider and they did have a good marriage. So, out of fear, no secrets.

Five women (36 percent) admitted that they kept secrets from their husbands, but these were always related to the welfare of the family. One woman said that her husband was a strict disciplinarian and, therefore, when the children needed anything, they went to her and she did not tell him about it. It appeared as if women did not keep "any other" secrets from their husbands and the reasons appeared to be that the men were the family economic providers and bringing home money for the family was a form of control over the family. In most of the women's responses it was clear that the traditional male dominance was an accepted part of their lives. It was clear, too, that loyalty to the spouse was an important factor in the responses. In some interviewees there appeared to be a sense of obligation as well as long-term responsibility for the bookkeeping of accrued obligations. To confess that a person had secrets from the partner was viewed negatively and thus contributed to the myth that married people should not keep secrets from each other.

Quarrels and Marriage

The question about quarrels that the couples had with each other brought out many feelings, particularly from the women. This could be because women are taught as children to practice self-control and not scream and yell. Many spouses believe that politeness, consideration and benevolence are important in a marriage and, not wishing to be rejected, some people may practice these arts unremittingly. If a person is kind, caring and loving all the time, I wondered subjectively, where is the zest in marriage? After all, a few quarrels may add spice to a meaningful situation. Moreover, people have competing tendencies, different interests, different ways of using time, and different biological rhythms, and therefore cannot always have the same desires, needs and wishes at the same time (Lederer and Jackson, 1968).

Conflicts are a natural part of life. How does a couple react to conflict? There are several ways in which a person could respond. If a person believes in the durability of a marriage, he or she will do what has to be done because the relationship should be strong enough to withstand disapproval or conflict. A number of women were defensive and responded with, "How dare you ask such a question?" By implication they were saying that they were good women and good women do not quarrel with their husbands. Thus I found that this question provoked anger in at least a few women. Only five of the women (36 percent) mentioned that they quarreled at all, and it varied from occasionally to rarely.

A major focus of quarrels was in-law relationships. The respondents' husbands were seen as spending too much time with relatives, or as providing financial support to their family of origin even if they had difficulty in providing for their own family. One woman mentioned that she quarreled with her husband every payday because he would spend a large part of his paycheck on drinking. Another woman simply said, "We quarreled about stupid money." One woman mentioned that they constantly quarreled about the children because he was too lenient. She did not want to discipline their sons because it was a man's job to make the sons into men. However, as the children grew older, their problems increased as they became more and more difficult to control. This led to nasty quarrels.

Among the men, seven (88 percent) admitted that they quarreled with their wives. I felt they were less defensive about this aspect of their lives than the women. What did the men quarrel about? One man said, "When I came home, all I wanted was peace and quiet and a hot meal on the table. I worked hard for it." But his wife would start complaining to him about the children, about his parents or about anything or everything—she certainly didn't make him feel peaceful. This constantly led to quarrels between them. The differences in attitude to the questioning about quarrels may reflect a cultural myth. Men can be masculine and quarrelsome whereas women are expected to be pleasant and cooperative. Women, therefore, felt threatened by such "impertinent" questioning.

Some of the questions involved the problem of trust. When spouses do not have any disagreements or quarrels, do they trust each other? How do these people who had been married for over 40 years on an average know what their spouses really thought and felt, if they were accommodating and thoughtful all the time? As Lederer and Jackson (1968) put it, for all anyone can tell, one spouse may secretly hate the other's guts.

Three women (21 percent) said that their marriages had lasted without quarrels. They had "good marriages" and it would be "wrong" to talk of minor quarrels. The issues appeared to be loyalty, fear of exposing their spouses, and the desire to present the family as a well-blended group. It appeared that there was a guilt-laden obligation to be loyal to their partners, who were dead in most cases. Common responses from this group were: "We had someone to provide for us." In the case of men: "There was someone to take care of us."

Sexual Relationships in Marriage

The question, "Do you believe that a good sexual relationship would result in a good marriage?," brought a number of reactions. Some thought that we were rude or crude in asking such questions, while others were amused. We found it easier to get responses from men than from women. The woman interviewer had fewer problems with this question than the man interviewer who was frowned upon when he attempted to ask women this question.

Six men (75 percent) said that they did have a good sexual relationship, whereas one said he did not. One mentioned that he did not bother his wife about sex for 15 years. The implication in this answer was that women did not like sex; men did and had to "bother" women for this purpose. One man mentioned that sex was the biggest thing in his marriage and the best part of it. Another man said that sex was an important part of marriage and added to its sanctity.

Women interviewees had a lot of difficulty because they felt that their privacy was being intruded upon. However six women (43 percent) responded by saying that they did their duty. One woman said that she participated in sex because she liked it. Another said that she would be honest—she really enjoyed sex, it was fun. One woman mentioned that she was sick most of the time and therefore sex was only a small part of their marriage. Her husband did not bother her because he knew that she was weak and ill most of the time—a myth that probably kept the marriage together and allowed each person to stay within it. Some women said that they were not sure if they had a good sexual relationship in their marriage. One woman specified that she did not want her husband to bother her with sex, so they slept in separate beds. She really believed that people should participate in sex only for procreation purposes and believed in the myth that sex was a man's perogative and women participated only to satisfy them. Of course, a good sexual relationship does not necessarily imply a good marriage and is only one aspect of it. The respondents' attitudes towards sex were a reflection of the older generation and of their social class which was one in which men were the providers and, therefore, controlled the family situation.

Extramarital Relations

Eighteen out of 25 respondents (72 percent) felt that extramarital relationships would not help a marriage. "You cannot build a marriage on deceit," one woman said, adding that, "It would create pain and jealousy in a relationship." One man said that too much of anything was not good. "If you had a wife, sex with her would be the most appropriate thing to do." Otherwise, he considered it to be a "sin." Another person specified that sex outside of marriage would shatter the trust that is a necessary ingredient of a workable marriage.

Trust is not something that one or the other spouse has as a personal quality or character trait. It is present between two individuals if it is warranted by their exchange of behavior. Stress, coupled with unclear communication or confusion, may temporarily affect and diminish the trust that exists between a couple, but the experience may fortify trust over the long run if they successfully handle the situation. Trust is developed over a period of time as a result of experience. If spouse Z's behavior is generally consistent and clear, spouse A will feel trust because he or she has learned to depend on this behavior. When two people can trust one another, each can relax for he or she knows what kind of behavior to expect and mutual confidence develops.

To the question, "Would an extramarital relationship lead to the breakdown of a marriage?" the answers, interestingly, were "No" by five out of 11 men (45 percent) though most felt that it would hurt a marriage. Six men (55 percent) felt that as long as it was discreet and did not cause problems in the marriage it was alright. One man added that this would be particularly true if the wife did not like sex. Among the women, six (43 percent) felt that extramarital relationships would not lead to the break-up of a marriage, though it could lead to conflicts and anger. Five women (36 percent) thought that it would lead to the break-up of a marriage because it would definitely cause a lot of pain and "Good Christians do not do such things."

Who Is the "Better" Person?

In marriages we also create myths that one is a better person than the other. Is this really true? Five men (63 percent) answered this question by saying that both spouses were really good people. One of them said that individually he and his wife were both good but it was their chemistry that caused problems for them. His wife was a good mother but beyond that, they did not have anything in common. One man mentioned that he had a bad marriage. He added that he can talk about it now, because his wife was dead and his sons lived away from him and rarely visited him. He mentioned that on one occasion, on his way to work, he had seen the picture of a beautiful woman on a billboard and had fantasies about her. At that point in his life, he met a woman with whom he had a brief affair. His wife was not aware of it and it was over in a short period. However, he felt guilty about it for a long period of time, but added he was discreet about it and it did not affect his marriage. His wife was definitely the better person.

Among the women six (43 percent) felt that both husband and wife were good people and were made for each other. Three women (21 percent) felt that the spouse was a better person either because he was ambitious to make the family more self-sufficient, better educated, or more widely traveled as in the case of a woman whose husband had been in the Navy. Another three women (21 percent) said that they were the better ones in the family because they took care of almost everything, including family finances. The rest of the women could not tell who they thought was the "better person" in the family.

CHILDREN AND FAMILY MYTHS

Why do couples have children? Is there a need to procreate or do children satisfy other needs in a couple? The question was: "Did you originally believe having a child meant having someone to love?" The answers revitalized my interest in myths. Seven out of eight men (88 percent) and 11 out of 14 women (78 percent) mentioned that they had children because they felt that they would have someone to love them always. Some mentioned that children were their own flesh and blood and came into this world through them; therefore, the children were obligated to love them. Some said that they loved their children very much and expected to receive the same kind of love from them.

Adult children were viewed as people who would offer them companionship in their old age. One woman mentioned that she had spent her whole life taking care of her husband and children and naturally expected her children to love her and be concerned about her in her old age. One man said that children help to hold the family together after the first few years of marriage.

A smaller percentage felt differently. They had children because they wished to reproduce themselves, but they did not expect children to love them, at least not completely. However they did feel that children should be respectful towards them because of the benefits and good rearing they had received.

Can a person demand love from anyone? Perhaps not, but parents can make children feel guilty if they do not respond as expected. Guilt could make adult children remain in contact, but a large number of them did not stay in constant touch. Visits were sporadic, with ritual visits during Thanksgiving and Christmas. The expectation that children should love parents because parents gave birth to them is a myth, for children do or do not love them, depending upon the way they experienced their parents.

Some of them mentioned that their children changed after getting married. Invariably, the husband, wife or in-laws were blamed for the loss of the adult child's affection or attention. One man mentioned that they had a great family relationship, until "HE"—the daughter's husband—entered the picture. It appeared that the daughter changed sides and was almost completely a member of her husband's household. "How could she do that?" hung heavily in the air. Of course it was a matter of loyalties as well. How loyal was she to her own old father? He was not like her, he had always loved his parents. A glazed look came into his eyes; it was an attempt to recall the essence of his childhood which, retrospectively, seemed to have been pleasurable. A feeling of being let down was present throughout the interview. With a sigh he added that his daughter had been fed, housed, sheltered, both physically and emotionally, comforted and protected; he could not understand why she was not completely loyal to him, particularly after his wife died. He expected her to be fair and to reciprocate his caring, that's all, nothing more, but it did not happen and he always thought about this and felt sad. Maybe children are not as wonderful as he thought they might be.

Other Reasons for Children

Seven out of eight men (88 percent) said that a family without children was no family at all. They felt that having children would enrich their lives and add meaning to it. One person felt that his family name should be continued and the best way to do this was through reproduction. He added, apologetically, that he felt sons were better than daughters. Since he was blessed with sons, his family name would continue. Though he was not wealthy, he was honest and hardworking and such families should continue to exist because hardworking people are needed in this country.

Among the women, 13 (93 percent) felt that they had some reason for having children. A few of the women mentioned that the children were not planned, but they learned to accept and love them. Some of them mentioned that the children were a joy or an enrichment in their lives. They commented that children gave them a purpose in life and often helped stabilize their marriage. One woman mentioned that she and her husband were from good, decent, hardworking families and they wanted their family name to continue. Therefore, they wished to have children who would fulfill this desire.

Martha indicated that she had had children because she loved her husband very much and this was the best way to show him that she loved him. Their children had done well in life, and she felt joy when she talked about them. The reasons for having children were blended with myths—children would enrich the parents' lives, they would be a joy, and so forth. Though interesting, these myths revealed a disparity, for not all of their children visited them or catered to their parents in their old age.

Leaving home and children, particularly after the death of their husbands, appeared to be particularly traumatic to some women. One woman had played the role of a wife and mother for a larger portion of her life. Most of the child-rearing responsibilities fell upon her shoulders as her husband worked away from home. She devoted herself exclusively to motherhood, and when her children left home, she faced a psychological void. After her husband died, she somehow expected to be taken care of by her children but was disappointed when she was brought to the nursing home. A feeling, "I had been let down," hung heavily in the air. "Nothing came out of having children, I did not really get much out of it. Life is painful," she added. One of her daughters whom she considered "nicer" might visit her but only when it was convenient for her. She added, with a slight smile, "I really don't know what life is all about." It appeared that in her case the myth of children being useful to parents had dissolved in reality.

Added to this, is the tremendous feeling of loneliness that these people have to face. Though the woman is freed from the concerns of child rearing, the empty nest crisis represents a turning point in her life, where she has to decide what to do with her life and her future with well over a quarter of century ahead of her if she remains in good health. This is especially true of the widowed housewife without the confidence or skills to make use of the new found leisure.

Children as Property

Did parents view children as a second chance for achievement? It was fascinating to note that seven men (88 percent) and a smaller percentage of women felt that children were their second opportunity to prove themselves: "I want my children to have what I did not have." Most men said that their children were better off than themselves; some said they belonged to the same status. Among the women, eleven (78 percent) mentioned that the child would not have to achieve for their sake. One woman mentioned that she did not want anything from her children except a few visits and an occasional phone call. Her view was, "We brought them into the world but they should achieve for themselves."

It could be that we touched upon a male myth in this situation which specified that men had to achieve in society. If fathers felt that they had not achieved in their lifetime, they wanted their sons to achieve. Usually parents mentioned that they had provided better opportunities for their children: "We gave them what we did not have," they said, and this varied from a good education, and a good home to fulfilling all their basic needs up to the time they could find jobs.

Most parents stated that they had been better parents to their children than their own parents had been to them. Many of them denied their own feelings of deprivation and made efforts to give their "all" to the children, coming across as the all-giving, sacrificing, martyred parent. In turn, the receiving child was bound to live up to the parent's expectations. For instance, one elderly man's son who became an engineer visited his father often, but could not keep him in his house because the father had a heart problem and needed constant care. With a working wife and two children, the son did not feel that he could take care of his father, but of course the obligation was clear that he had to visit his father as often as possible.

I felt that individuals who lived up to their parents' expectations and did achieve were left, particularly in the case mentioned, with a feeling of obligation and indebtedness to the parent that could never be repaid. The strings that are attached to such martyred giving has endless repercussions. Whenever the father felt slightly indisposed, he called his son who, in spite of his responsibilities at work or at home, would be there at his call. Feelings regarding a child's indebtedness are so exaggerated that there is no hope for repayment. It appears as if children are fixated in these loyal, guilt-laden relationships (Boszormenyi-Nagy, 1965b).

Fifty years ago, the role of a man and father was that of chief provider; this was particularly true of the blue collar, retired workers studied. They did not achieve much in their lives and felt the need for their children to do better. In the working class subculture, conformity and obedience seemed to be the rule (Komarovsky, 1964). Though men mentioned that they wanted their sons to achieve, the division of labor was clear in the family: Most of the child-rearing responsibility belonged to the mother; if achievement and education were to be encouraged, it was the mother's function. Yet career commitment in those days was stereotypically masculine rather than feminine; the son did not have a strong occupational role model in socialization if the father withdrew from family participation. A consistent research finding showed that the son's identification with the father was a critical antecedent for occupational interest development (Komarovsky, 1964). However, the mother became an important figure for identification.

Children and Obligations

Seven men (88 percent) and 12 women (81 percent) mentioned that children were obligated to them in different ways. One man said, "We are parents, after all, and they do owe us love, respect and obedience whenever it is necessary." One man said, "We took care of them and they owe us something." Only one man said his children did not owe him anything: "You brought them into the world but its up to the children. If they decide that they wish to take care of parents, it is really good. If not, you could just say that you are not lucky!" Several women mentioned that they would like their children to be respectful towards them. One woman mentioned that her children visited her only on festive days as an obligation. Though the respondent cared about them deeply, they were late to come and quick to leave. There is a myth present that indicates that "If you are my flesh and blood, you should love me, irrespective of how good or bad I was, simply because I am your parent. If you do not love me or are not respectful towards me, regardless of what I did to you, you are a bad child."

The Favorite Child

Which child did the parent like best? Was there a child who could be distinguished as the respondent's favorite? The men appeared to like their sons more than their daughters. Four out of eight men (50 percent) mentioned that they loved their sons more, particularly their firstborn. "He was the first child," "There was something special about him," and "He was the best" were among the statements made in support of their feelings. Among the women, four (29 percent) mentioned their oldest child, irrespective of sex, as the favorite because this was their firstborn. One woman who mentioned her oldest daughter as her favorite added that she could not stand her second daughter because she was arrogant and defiant. One woman specified that she gave up on her oldest child because she was an unpleasant person, but considered her second and third children to be her favorites.

Those who reported loving all their children equally mentioned that one could not distinguish among children. "If you parent children, you love them equally." When they were asked to think in terms of whom they found easy to be with, they reacted with, "You cannot ask us that question, they are all our children. Its not fair." This is the myth of parents loving all children equally. They did not wish to offend their adult children and they also wanted to live up to the myth of being a perfect parent and thus not distinguish their feelings between children.

Those families with a favorite child also gave the child a role assignment that described the child as perfect or ideal. The function of the favorite child appeared to vary in the family from that of a healer or parentified and loyal child to a burden bearer. However, in most cases the favorite children were also pets of their families. They did not cause the family any troubles. They added color and happiness to the family in terms of never hurting or annoying any particular family member. The favorite child's goodness and nondemanding behavior was used as a model against the siblings who expressed their negative feelings.

If this favorite child feels any anger or depression, it is kept under cover because she or he is not supposed to be upset. The inner needs and feelings of this child were often negated, denied, or minimized. He or she was the best and had to live up to the family's expectations. The favorite child performs a major family function—to reflect affection and acceptance back to parents, constantly and loyally. Often these children live up to the images that parents create so that their own emotional needs are often overlooked (Boszormenyi-Nagy, 1965a). As seen in this study, the favorite child also becomes the parentified child and takes over the responsibility of caring for or visiting the older parents wherever they may live.

MYTHS REGARDING RELATIONSHIPS WITH CHILDREN AND IN-LAWS

It appears that families have overt and implicit myths that they create regarding expectations of loyalty from their members and these are incorporated into different family members' behavior. Based upon the myths that are part of their lives, adults and

children live their life course. "I am a happy person," "I suc-
ceed in everything I do," "I cannot have fun, " etc., are injunc-
tions to which children are exposed. These become part of their
lives and they live up to the myth as it creates a role and in one
way or another develops coherence for the family.

Specific roles are created for family members. One man described his son as being wild and his daughter as mild. He stated
that they were opposites when they were young and they continue to be the same, even now. He was more fond of his daughter, but the "wild" son was his wife's favorite. He added that
his son would lose his temper at the slightest provocation. This
would make the father angry, but his wife would side with the
son and somehow smooth matters over for all of them. He sighed.
Those days, though painful at times, also held much pleasure
for him; he had good memories of them. Of course, his son did
not change. He got married and was divorced, and this did not
surprise anyone. He added that his daughter was mild because
"She was a girl, you know," implying that girls were easier to
deal with than boys. This was another myth—of women being
mild, which was a traditional way of viewing them.

Rules of Behavior in the Family

Family rules are either implicit or explicit. In addition, they
allow for modulation of energy so as to control or limit relationships, as well as to allow intimacy. Rules perpetuate themselves
and reproduce. Each family has its own rules of good behavior
for which family members get rewarded and gain approval. It
also has rules against poor or bad behavior for which family
members receive disapproval. For instance, in some families being lazy could be equivalent to a crime, whereas in other families,
being lazy is accepted but telling lies would be strongly re-
proached. Seven men (88 percent) mentioned that they had strict
rules of behavior in their families. No bad behavior was allowed
and if anyone misbehaved, particularly when they were young,
the father dealt with them. If it involved simple interactions, the
mother handled it. Most parents believed in spanking their chil-

dren. They believed that if you spared the rod you did spoil the child. It was not viewed as abuse, but as punishment sufficient to make the child think about his or her behavior and change it quickly. All respondents seemed to have a strong sense of what they considered to be right and wrong.

Based upon their family myths, the respondents set up rules which they hoped would become ingrained in their children's behavior. Talking back to adults was completely disapproved of by all the adult members. Most of the men mentioned that there was no one in their family who could be described as negative or bad. Also there was a kind of pride: "We had good children and their problems were very minor." Another aspect of the family's qualities also became apparent—the loyalty of the parents toward their adult children.

Among the women, one came out with the response that her husband was the bad one in the family. He was immoral and started fooling around with other women a few months after he married her. She felt that there was no remedy for this and she could not control his behavior because he was a much older man, but she described herself and her daughter as "good people." Another woman described her older daughter as bad. She learned to fool her mother and father at a young age and would spend her time with boys, rather than at school. As soon as she was old enough, she went away with a boy whom she later married and divorced. She had been through three divorces so far, was a heavy smoker and drinker, and would outcurse anyone in the world. She was a "bad" girl and her mother hoped that one day she would repent her bad behavior and become a good Christian once more. She was angry, but also felt sorry for her because she believed that her daughter had ruined her own life. Of course there was nobody else like her in the family. She was unusual and different—not at all like her other daughter who was a quiet person.

At times roles in the families are based upon myths where adults and children are assigned to assume inappropriate generational and sexual roles. Instead of being experienced as distinct entities with the full range of feelings and attitudes, some of these individuals are experienced as incomplete entities and they are responded to by other family members as if they were partial human beings having only singular characteristics. The constellation of roles allows internal conflicts of each member to be acted out within the family rather than within the self, and each family member attempts to deal with his or her own conflicts by changing the other (Olson and Sprenkle, 1976).

Children who are overtly good, quiet, and conforming may often be assigned parental responsibilities. Such role assignments are shifted readily. Parents who are unable psychologically to be parents may justify their inability under the guise of being permissive, democratic, and nonauthoritarian. Parentification of children may ensue as a result of parental inactivity, inertia, or chaotic behavior which amounts to emotional abdication by the parents. The feelings that permeate the relationship in these families are depression, despair, rage, or sadness (Boszormenyi-Nagy and Spark, 1973).

Head of the Family

Who was the head of the family in the real sense of the word? Who controlled the money, the household activities, and so forth in the family? Six men (75 percent) said that they were the head of the family. They provided the family with money, food, clothing, and shelter. They paid the bills and did everything for the family members. Naturally, most of the family power rested in their hands. Among the women, nine (64 percent) mentioned that the man was the head of the family; the chief reason they specified was economics. In these situations, the head of the family was the family provider. The goals of child rearing were essentially in the woman's hands and the aim was to rear them to be become ''good Christians'' so that children would lead honest, decent lives. There was no power (influence and control) connected with housework, which most of the women did.

The power structure of the family could be classified into husband-dominated, wife-dominated, and egalitarian types. In the husband-dominated type, the wife performed all the household duties. The belief in these lower income families is that the father is the head of the family because he is the chief wage earner. Such families are generally perceived to be more patriarchial than middle class families (Komarovsky, 1964). There is another view which indicates that lower class families are more matriarchial but I believe that they become matriarchial by default, due to the fact that either the husband is an alcoholic or is not a good provider. One man mentioned that he and his wife were both the head of the family. They had an egalitarian relationship where both husband and wife made joint decisions, and they appeared to be happy with this arrangement. One woman also mentioned that her marriage was egalitarian in that they made joint decisions.

Family and Sickness

To the question, "Was there any member of the family who was constantly ill?" six out of eight men (75 percent) and 11 women (81 percent) mentioned that no one was ill in the family. One man indicated that his daughter was ill most of the time. He and his wife had to spend a lot of time with her and provide her with all kinds of medical help but she never really got completely well. She was just a weak person and the family learned to accept her as such.

Another man mentioned that his son used to pretend to be ill. This was painful for him and his wife as his son turned out to be almost a "bum." The son hated to work and found a number of excuses for staying at home and pretending that he was sick. This created some friction between the interviewee and his wife as she was protective of her son and encouraged him to be lazy. He added that there was no cure for laziness, though there were different remedies for all kinds of illnesses.

The myth of illness is utilized unconsciously in families, often to keep the family together. Actually, the problem is not likely to be with one individual but with the family as a system. Faulty interactional patterns might cause the family a lot of agony and pain. In such cases the solutions that the family have attempted are likely to be stereotyped repetitions of ineffective transactions, which only generate heightened affect without producing change (Ferreira, 1963).

Extended Family Influences

The extended family and in-laws of those interviewed appeared to have a dramatic influence on them. The existence of these elderly people centered around relatives, all the more because there were so few competing social ties or interests. Anxiety over family problems and shame over some behavior constitute a large part of the memories of these older people. As Komarovsky (1964) noted in her study, "Your relatives can hurt you more than anybody because you love them most."

How did the men get along with their in-laws? Six men (75 percent) described their in-laws as "good," "decent," and "fine" people. One man described his in-laws as being ambitious people who were constantly pushing their children to higher achievements. The rest of the men did not seem to have good feelings about their in-laws. It appeared that there was reciprocity in this respect. When the in-laws did not like the son-in-law, he in turn disliked them and they kept their distance while the daughter continued to keep in touch with her parents. The wife's emotional involvement with her mother continued to remain strong; accordingly, the men had to adjust themselves to this relationship.

Among the married women, six (43 percent) mentioned that they liked their in-laws. Women's attitudes towards their in-laws appeared to be tolerant. This could be due to the fact that the daughters usually lived closer to their own parents and had minimal contact with their husband's parents, which made it easier for them to be more tolerant and less critical of them.

Did the attitude of the parents-in-law influence the manner in which the wives were treated? In all the cases the daughters-in-law were approved of and liked by the man's parents. It almost appeared to be a taboo to say that the wife was not liked. Among the women, eleven (78 percent) indicated that their husbands were approved of and liked by their parents.

What roles did in-laws play in the life of these families? Among the married men and women, eleven mentioned that they were involved with in-laws. They visited them frequently and almost everything that was done in the family was discussed with them. As Komarovsky (1964) specifies, the economic aid that the relatives give is not as important as the social role they play. In a few families, being with relatives was the sole social experience of group membership. One-third never spent any time with another couple and some of them were completely isolated. The church was the only arena outside the family where they developed social relationships.

Except for one man who said that he was not bothered by his in-laws, the rest responded either by saying that they were somewhat or too involved with their in-laws. There was also the myth that the wives, however old they were, needed their mothers because they were the best people to give advice and help the daughters through their problems. The men preferred that the wives go to their mothers who ''really cared'' about the welfare of their children rather than to outsiders who might gossip about them or give their wives ''bad advice.'' The men were not as closely involved with their families of origin as their wives were. This does not mean that they were uninvolved or unconcerned about the welfare of their relatives. However, in the long run they appeared to have become closer to the in-laws.

The interviewees visited their parents or parents-in-law more frequently than the parental generation visited them. This seemed to contradict the popular belief that parents and parents-in-law try to interfere with or break into the family boundaries of the married couple, although parents did ''take sides'' with their own children whenever matters went out of hand. Interference as understood in middle class circles did not break or destroy the marriage. It was as if one more member was added to the family; if the person was disliked, he or she was overlooked. The culture of the blue collar families appeared to include a larger number of relatives from the extended family.

What was the relationship of these adult children (the present elderly) with their own parents? Did these adults live up to the image that was created of them by their parents when they were young? Do children live up to roles that parents create for them? I found that all the adult men and women remembered the roles they had played. Most of the women described themselves as good and quiet people, except one woman who mentioned that she should have listened to her parents and not married her husband who was a "bum." She was considered to be an uncontrollable person by her parents and that is how she behaved.

Among the men, one described himself as the "cute, spoiled child" and that was the way he lived his life. He enjoyed life, was fairly irresponsible, and lost out on his family life. It appeared that roles created for children are powerful, and the family of origin had the power to indoctrinate children. Long after the parents were dead and gone, the children still lived up to them: "My father said" or "my mother said," "This is the way I was" were constant phrases.

In the next few chapters the life histories of four elderly members will be presented and we will witness how myths are woven in and out through their family lives.

CHAPTER 3

In the Life of Emily Crosby

Every family has a dance that is uniquely its own. Dance is thought made manifest through movement rhythms. Dance is a point of view in its styles, and a language in its forms and techniques. Dance techniques are the grammars of movements that have been developed in various cultures. Every family culture also develops its own rhymes and rhythms and family members through practice build up patterns to suit the particular family dance. Now, let us enter Emily's family and the dance they perform.

"I knew you were coming," was the way I was greeted by this tall, buxom, silver-haired, blue-eyed woman. Her voice was loud and clear. Thus I settled with Emily in her room, she comfortable in her large chair and myself lost in the cushiony folds of a large armchair.

EARLY HISTORY

Emily was the oldest child in a family of four daughters. Her maternal grandparents from her mother's side came to the United States a few months before Emily's mother Pamela was born. Pamela had six sisters and one brother. Emily's father Peter came to the United States from Poland when he was 16 years of age.

FAMILY TREE OF EMILY CROSBY

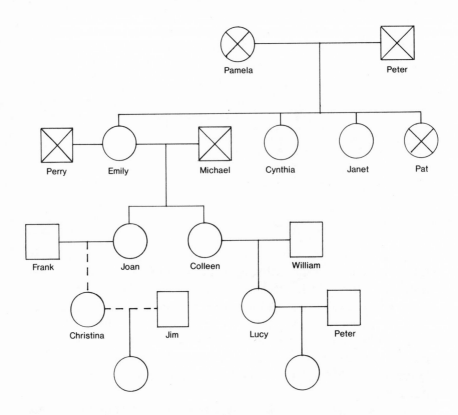

He was accompanied by his younger sister who remained a life-long friend of Emily. Peter's knowledge of English was limited. Pamela and Peter married in their early twenties. "How was life?" I asked Emily. "Oh, it was terrible, you know, my mother had a bad life, because of my father, he was not a good man."

Peter worked on the railroad while Pamela stayed home and gave birth to babies. After four children their life changed. Peter started to come home late at night and was almost always drunk. There was constant strife in the family. Pamela was not able to make both ends meet, so she started to work too. She was a cleaning woman and spent a lot of her time away from home. Emily, the oldest child, was inducted into playing the role of mother and caretaker for her three younger sisters, Cynthia, Janet and Pat. Emily's father could not read or write English and, therefore, his wife would spell out words on paper, including the time he should be at work. Pamela constantly complained that he was useless, because he could not speak English fluently and also because she had to help him in every way when he went to work. All he wanted, she complained, was sex.

Often at night Emily would hear her parents quarreling and then Pamela would move into her daughter's cot. Their home consisted of two rooms, with the kitchen converted to a bedroom for the two older children at night. Pamela would complain that her husband was bothering her about sex and fight with him, loudly. Emily would listen to their fights and find it difficult to go back to sleep.

As time passed Peter spent more and more time away at work. Paydays he would come home late and often drunk. There were angry quarrels that would drive him out of the house. The mother would complain that he came home because he wanted only one thing—sex.

Tragedy struck this family when Peter was 42 years of age. He was late for work one day and took a shortcut through the railroad tracks where a train was stationed. He had almost crossed between the cars when the train began to move and his legs were cut off. Before much help could be given, he had bled to death. Emily noted that it was horrible. They brought her father's body home and placed it in a coffin; the severed legs were wrapped up and placed next to the body. He was no good, but it was tragic when he died. They kept the body in the coffin for a whole night before he was buried. A number of friends came to view the body and pay their respects.

A strange incident took place at that time. The youngest daughter Pat, who was 12 years of age, was watching the mourners come and go when she suddenly screamed loudly. Her sisters found her in the yard, looking terrified as if she had seen a ghost. Later they found out that someone had attempted to rape her. After that incident Pat stopped talking. She would sit in a corner, staring at the walls or ceiling. She made no effort to go to school and died while still in her teens. Emily added, "I think she was crazy."

After Peter's death, Pamela spent most of her time outside the home as a laundress for other people. At times she would bring home clothes and wash them till late at night. The rooms they lived in smelled of soap. Then she would iron the clothes till early morning. She did not remarry. There was no time for anything except to make both ends meet. Meanwhile, Emily and her sisters attended a Polish catholic school; Emily dropped out after the fifth grade.

THE FAMILY MYTH

The myth in the family said that men were bad people interested only in exploiting women for sexual purposes. It appeared that there was a conflict of interest among the men and women and this tug of war set up alignments between the women against the men.

Though the family myth I constantly heard said that men were bad, it was obvious that there was much strife in this family among the women as well. While Pamela was away, Emily was in charge of the family, but there was constant fighting among the sisters.

Quarreling

Quarreling was an accepted mode of behavior in this family. Anger was expressed in different ways, ranging from mere change of facial expression to a self-consummating outpouring, accompanied by shouting, obscenity, blows or violence. In this family, physical violence was accepted as necessary and there was a great deal of blaming. Blaming someone else was a way of attacking someone or defending oneself against someone, but quarrels become especially bitter when the antagonists raked up the past or anticipated the future. Quarrels in the family were essentially a transitory burst of anger in which people felt themselves attacked and retaliated to defend themselves. When the quarrel is set largely by the factors mentioned, the quality of the accompanying anger is determined also by how the issue is perceived and the quality of the anger in turn affects the course of the quarrel (Henry, 1965).

One day, while Emily was in charge, her sister Cynthia provoked her into a fight, as often happened. She added that this was a common occurrence, particularly with Cynthia who wanted more freedom than her sisters. But Emily was strict with her sisters, carrying out her mother's orders. The fight got violent. The sisters started to hit each other and in the process they used every object as a weapon at hand. Before Emily knew it, she was banging doors and screaming at the top of her voice. At one point she felt that they would really harm each other physically, so she ran out of the house and slammed the door so angrily that the glass dropped out of it onto the ground. The mother was extremely upset because the window had to be replaced at substantial cost. Emily felt bad because she knew how hard her mother worked for their money. Emily and Cynthia did not talk to each other for a long time, leaving scars of pain and anger though she could not remember exactly why the quarrel started. This seemed to be true of this family. There was a lot of violence in the culture of this family and what family members remembered was not the reasons for fighting but the violence that went with it. This fighting did stop when there was damage to physical property, though verbal abuse and mild physical fighting continued to be a part of the family behavior.

Strife and struggle for existence appeared to be a way of life for this family. Caring and doing things together were at a minimum. Sex was shrouded in mystery, because it was not proper to talk about such matters. In this manner, the daughters were kept ignorant even of menstruation. Thus, when Emily menstruated for the first time, it came as a shock to her. She thought that she was bleeding to death. Her mother had gone out to work, so Emily ran from the bathroom to her aunt who lived in the front portion of their house and told her, "I am bleeding, I am going to die." Her aunt assured her that such was not the case and gave her a piece of diaper to wear, advising her to speak to her mother when she returned home. Emily did, but her mother gave her more diapers and told her that this would happen to her every month. That was all the knowledge she had of menstruation; she was not told its meaning. Sex was a taboo topic in this family. Emily raised herself up with dignity and told me, "We could not talk about sex." She went on to criticize the present generation and the way young women behave.

Individual Sex-Role Patterns in the Family

Identification with parents is a two-step procedure. As the process begins, children of both sexes usually make an initial identification with their mother, following which boys change their identification and model with the father while girls maintain the mother as a primary model. Successive identification has been described by Parsons (1970).

There are some problems in defining human sex roles. The nature and development of sex role from a social-learning approach was aptly summarized by Sutton-Smith, Rosenberg and Morgan (1972) who indicated that masculinity and femininity are not simply the result of birth as a boy or a girl. The gender role that is assigned to the child at birth is based on his/her biological sex, and the child is subsequently treated as a member of that sex. In accordance with this cultural prescription, different attitudes are evidenced toward children of different sexes and different behaviors of these children are reinforced. A set of rules is established for the child based on gender (sex role) and the aim of the parent is to provide those reinforcements which are conducive to the adoption and assimilation of that role.

A family and its structure have an effect on how sex role patterns are developed in that family. Besides identification with the parent, the original biological differences are overlaid by many response systems that are sustained according to their appropriateness with other family members, peers, teachers, and the opposite sex (Willi, 1982).

In Emily's family, the sex roles that members played would unfold as we proceeded with the story as related by Emily. She claimed that the women were viewed only as sex objects by their men and men were viewed as the aggressors by the women. Women responded to the men's needs with compliance, but they did not enjoy sex.

Though Emily stated in no uncertain terms that sex was a taboo topic in the family, her explanations, discussions and way of looking at sex were explicit. Whenever the occasion arose, she would graphically describe how one person, a family member or a neighbor, behaved sexually. Though the implicit family rule appeared to say: *Do not discuss sex in the family*, there appeared to be a preoccupation with this subject in every discussion we had.

Marriage and Family Living

When Emily was 18, she started to date. At first she dated a young man who was controlling and domineering; then she dropped him for a kind and loving Irishman, Michael, whom she married. She was 20 at that time and her mother advised her not to marry Michael because she saw in him all the signs of an alcoholic. Of course, Emily paid no attention to her. She was very much in love and wanted to be this man's wife. She added that in those days women and men did not live together as they do nowadays, and sex was not looked on as fun as it is now. If a person wanted to have sex, they had to get married; thus, she married Michael.

Her wedding night was celebrated at her house. She was very frightened of her husband and requested of him, ''Please, don't hurt me.'' Emily described her first married night in great detail and, I suspect, got great pleasure in doing so. However, she ended up by telling me that sex was only for men and that women participated in it merely to please them. Her marriage appeared to be rosy for a few months and then she noticed that her husband drank more than he should every day. She would fight with him over this and the fighting would escalate until he left the house in anger.

Emily became the mother of two daughters, Joan and Colleen, within a short period of time. Meanwhile, the stress in the marriage appeared to be increasing constantly. Her husband would spend a lot of money on drinking and gambling. There were paydays when he would not bring his paycheck home and he would be found lying on the outside porch or at their neighbor's door.

Emily became more and more upset by her husband's behavior. She realized she had the best weapon—SEX. She would refuse to go to bed with him, saying that she had a headache, because she wanted to get back at him for not providing for the family. If he did not bring home money, she did not want to have anything to do with him. Thus, sex became a reward or punishment strategy for her. She added that, "In those days it wasn't as it is today." There were no contraceptives and "If you were lucky you did not get pregnant."

Her life situation slowly deteriorated. Michael became more alcoholic and created problems for her and the family. She added, "I told you earlier, men are no good and my husband was not a good man either," except that he did not beat her or hurt her physically. He was oblivious of the fact that he had parented two children. Colleen, the younger daughter, was vocal and combative and would make matters unpleasant, if she was angry. Late one night, as usual, her father came home drunk and demanded that his food be warmed up. Emily refused and he got furious and started to abuse her verbally, throwing dishes on the floor. Emily became frightened but Colleen lost her temper. She started to scream and yell at her father and before anyone knew it they were in a physical struggle. This was the first time the father had hit his daughter. She was then a teenager. Colleen started to hit him back and all hell broke loose. Colleen had always been her mother's supporter.

Emily wiped her eyes; she was crying as she talked to me. It was such a bad incident. I asked about her older daughter, Joan. Emily said that both her daughters disliked their father and kept their distance from him. They knew he was no good. (No one understood that he suffered from a disease called alcoholism.) Thus, Michael was the outsider and the "bad guy" in the family. An outsider is a person who is disqualified from full social acceptance due to some stigma that is attached to him or her. In this case, Michael's stigma was his drinking and his violent temper which gave him a poor moral status in the eyes of his wife and children.

There was also triangulation in the family. Bowen (1976) suggests that no matter how chaotic triadic behaviors may look in a family, these behaviors are nevertheless proceeding along limited and almost preordained pathways. Bowen believes that when a family has been together for a long time, the process of triangling goes through such a fixed chain reaction that it has a sequence.

While Emily described the violence that was present between her husband and herself, I wondered how many wives and husbands ever let the other know how anger affects them? Sometimes, Emily would be so frightened that she would react to her husband with complete dependency, which was also a reflection on her self-esteem. But there were instances where she would provoke him and her best weapon appeared to be refusal to have sex. Even while she was telling this, I could sense anger, fear, pain, revulsion, as well joy in the control that she had over him. However, between the two of them the basic meaningful relationship was negated as the intensity of the struggle increased without limit, and the restraint imposed by the relationship-feeling was destroyed, permitting fights to develop as between enemies. But the terrible part was that these people were not enemies and the very condition of fighting required that they have common interests. Emily discussed how each behaved during a quarrel and described how she felt after it was over. She came out with the comment, "He was just like my father, no good." Later, while she was describing a few of the fights, she came out in anger, "He was a foul-mouthed, mad-dog, out-of-the-gutter man and life was difficult."

There appeared to be strong alliances between the mother and her two daughters just as there had been strong alliances between Emily's mother and her daughters. This family showed two different family styles. Relationships with the father appeared as if they belonged to a disengaged family with a relative absence of strong connections; the relationship ties between father and children were weak. On the other hand, the mother and her daughters formed a part of an enmeshed family that resembled an error-activated system with high resonance between the parts.

The enmeshed family was characterized by a "tight interlocking" of its members. Their quality of connectedness was such that attempts on the part of one member to change elicited swift complementary resistance on the part of the others (Minuchin and Fishman, 1982). One of the effects of enmeshment is to weaken the boundaries that allow family subsystems to work. Frequently, the boundary between the nuclear family and families of origin is not well maintained. The boundary separating parents from their children is frequently invaded in improper ways. The roles of spouse and parent are never clearly differentiated so that neither the spouse subsystem nor the parent subsystem can operate with ease. Finally, the children are not differentiated on the basis of age or maturational level; therefore, the sibling subsystem cannot contribute properly to the socialization process (Minuchin and Fishman, 1982). The family roles that Emily's daughters developed were restricted predominately to being friendly and helpful to the mother.

Boundaries at the abstract level can also be rules that regulate information, access, and activity in such a way as to exclude different members from certain aspects of different subsystems. Thus, when the father is talked about, his bad behavior is shared as open knowledge between the two children who are close to the mother, and the father is treated constantly as an outsider. This implicit rule regulates information and creates a real boundary between all members of the family. If the children started to become the father's allies, then the rules of the family would change, but this did not happen. Within the mother and daughters' relationship, the members were overly responsive to one another, as well as extremely dependent upon one another. The women in the family needed each other—to disagree, to agree and to emphasize differences. Firm and flexible boundaries preserve the differentiation of the family; these were absent in the Crosby household.

Communication

Communication is part of the family culture; through the interaction of personalities, roles and genders in the family, different types of messages are given to family members. As we are aware, communication is one of the major channels for regulating subsystems and boundaries. Communication also refers to verbal and nonverbal behavior in a social context. Thus it can be said that communication is more than just talking. A person's gestures, posture, movements, silences, facial expressions, tone of voice, and manner of dress are all communicative.

All messages that people receive have two key components. The most obvious aspect of the message is the content, that is, the information the sender wishes to transmit. But there is also a more subtle level of communication which is intended to influence the behavior of the receiver. People who send messages desire a response from the receiver and the request is built into all messages (Weakland, 1976). The message is aimed at influencing the receiver to respond in a desired manner. Thus, each message affects and is affected by the relationship between the sender and the receiver.

If the content of a statement fully expresses its intent or ''request,'' then there is little room for confusion. A simple question such as, ''What time is it?'' can be asked in an entirely straightforward manner and be aimed solely at obtaining a factual response. At times, when the purpose is not explicitly or clearly disclosed, interpersonal misfiring could be the result (Haley, 1978).

In this family there was poor communication in terms of clarity, consistency, openness, and directness, along with alliances and subgroupings. The family myth appeared to say that men were bad, that all they needed from women was sex. While this kept the men busy, the women covered their own flaws by their supportive attitudes towards each other and negative attitudes towards men.

Sisters' Marriages

Emily's younger sister, Janet, also dated an alcoholic and married him against everyone's advice. Though she was close to her sisters and mother, when it came to her choice of a husband she would not listen to them. She hoped to change her husband after they were married. However, this did not happen and her life became as miserable as Emily's. The other surviving sister, Cynthia, was described as sensible because she did not marry for a long period of time. However, when she did marry at age 40, she too did not listen to anyone and married a man who was divorced and also an alcoholic. She informed her family that he "just drinks a little," but he turned out to be an alcoholic, and a gambler as well. Soon all her lifetime savings had disappeared.

The three sisters had one thing in common—alcoholic husbands. This left the women close to each other. They all hated men. How could this have happened? Perhaps these women "conspired" among themselves to have "negative" husbands and thus avoid having to face up to problems among themselves? These marriages could also have provided an opportunity for the women to show that they were the better people in the family, for the women handled not only the housework but all household responsibilities as well. In reality, they were controlling women, who chose alcoholic men as husbands.

In all marital relationships the power structure of the family can generally be described as husband dominated, wife dominated, or egalitarian. In this family, the strength of the women arose from their joint personal resources and their togetherness. They were strong personalities married to weak men.

All families and people who have a history together follow organized ways of behaving with one another. Everyone is capable of learning and becoming organized. To be organized is to follow patterned, redundant ways of behaving and to exist in a hierarchy. People who organize together form a power ladder in which each person has a place in the hierarchy. Hierarchies evolve through sequences that occur in the organization. A structure is composed of repeated acts among people (Haley, 1978). The women chose men whose alcoholism kept them out of the family system or on its periphery. Thus, the women became the controllers of the family in terms of power, though the men provided them with money. As Komarovsky (1964) indicates in her study of blue-collar workers, the dominance of women led the husbands to rage, violence, frequent absence from home, and perhaps infidelity, all of which were reactions of weak husbands who could neither accept defeat nor settle for half a loaf. These men turned away from home and had negative attention focused on them.

LATER YEARS

While her daughters were growing up, Emily kept the constructive discussion of sex completely out of the family. Did Emily's children get any information about menstruation? Emily smiled, "Just like my mother, I did not tell them anything, they were good girls." Ignorance is bliss. When they went on dates, they came back home at the given time. The older daughter, Joan, dated a man who reminded Emily of her husband and she advised her daughter not to marry him. But as happened between Emily and her mother, her daughter would not listen to her and got married to an alcoholic named Frank. As Emily predicted, the marriage was on the rocks within a month as he was not only an alcoholic but also a womanizer.

Joan was miserable but found her happiness with her sister Colleen and mother Emily. Joan would visit home often and complain about her husband while Emily would be very supportive.

It happened once again, when the younger daughter, Colleen, married. At least this man hardly drank, Colleen told her mother. However, after they were married, he started to spend more and more money on drinking. The same family dance started all over again. The steps and rhythms of the dance were still similar to those of two generations ago.

Death of Emily's Husband

When Emily was in her early fifties, her husband developed cancer of the liver and was ill for a long period of time. The day he died, Emily sat on a chair reading her Bible. As she was reading, he died; she felt death pass right through her. One of her greatest supports was her husband's sister, Margaret, who not only gave her money but was a source of tremendous emotional support throughout this rocky marriage. There was a close, stable coalition between them and a rigidly bound collusion against Margaret's older brother, Emily's husband Michael. She was her brother's only sister and so, in many ways, the support systems from his family of origin belonged to his wife and not to him.

Michael's death was sad but Emily felt that she could manage on her own. She had worked as a cleaning woman off and on and felt that she could still function in this manner. She reminisced about him. There had been a lot of teasing and taunting about sex. He always wanted sex. This was how men were and she was relieved that the marriage was over.

Death of Emily's Mother

Emily started to work as a cleaning woman and dated men as well. At this time, her mother, Pamela, who was in her early eighties, became ill. She was living in her daughter Janet's house since Emily could not afford to take care of her. When her mother got too weak and knew that she was about to die, Emily visited her mother in her sister's house and sat watching her from a large armchair. She reminisced about their life; then she got tired of sitting and lay down next to her mother on the bed. She gave her mother some water to drink. Emily was tired; as she was about to doze off, she heard a funny choking sound. She turned over and touched her mother and called out, "Ma, ma, are you alright?" but there was no response. After a few minutes she called out to her sister who mentioned that normally after a drink of water their mother went to sleep; so Emily came back and laid down to rest.

About half an hour passed in complete silence. Emily was uncomfortable. She called out to her sister again, and this time her sister's husband came along and he placed a mirror in front of the mother's nose and declared her dead. Emily was terrified. She had diarrhea for a long period of time and had difficulty in attending the funeral. She felt that "Death had just passed through her" for a second time. However, this time, though scary, painful and morbid, it was alright; she had always been her mother's favorite child and aptly she was in her mother's bed when she passed away.

Emily's Remarriage

After the death of her husband and mother, Emily was in a depression. She went to see a soothsayer, which was a customary practice in their family. She claimed that she did not really believe what the soothsayer said, but contradicted her own statement by saying that whatever happened in her life had been predicted by soothsayers. When she was a young girl, she was told that she would be married and have two children. This turned out to be true. Once again she decided to see what the future held for her. The soothsayer predicted that she would be remarried in a short time. Emily was pleased since she needed the economic support.

In Emily's life, there appeared to be a belief in superstitions as well as in fortune telling. When asked what superstitions the family believed in, Emily mentioned that it was generally accepted by everyone that when a black cat crosses their path it brings them bad luck. Walking under a ladder was also considered to be bad luck. What would they do if a black cat did cross their path? They would retrack their steps backwards a few feet away and then proceed to walk ahead. Bad luck might include anything from having a bad day to suffering a major disaster.

After the soothsayer's prediction of remarriage, Emily got really serious about looking for a man—which means that it did influence the manner in which she thought. She met a few men and settled down to dating one person named Perry. After a few dates, she found that he drank a lot, but she did not pay much attention to this. At this time, her older daughter warned her that her man friend had all the appearances of an alcoholic. Just as her daughters did not listen to her when they chose their mates, and just as Emily had not listened to her mother when she married her first husband, now Emily did not heed the advice. She felt that she was the mother, older and wiser, and therefore her daughter did not have any right to give her advice about whom to date or marry.

Once again, this is a fascinating phenomenon in this family: The women cling to each other in all matters except when choosing a mate; then they get aggressively independent. Their choice of a mate may be poor, but they stay with it and do not take advice. They become self-righteous and there is denial of their need to marry a weak or alcoholic man. These marriages also fulfilled the protective and defensive functions of these families. The family rule for three generations was that men are to blame for everything that goes wrong in the family; the second rule indicated that women support each other. The overt family myth said that men were bad and aggressive, whereas subconsciously women chose men whom they could control. At the same time it gave the women leverage to keep their contact with the family of women close-knit and tight.

Thus, Emily dated her second husband, a divorced Polish man who had come to the United States when he was in his teens. He had a daughter by a former wife. Emily's older daughter, Joan, mentioned that he could not be a "good man" because his former wife, whom Joan had met once, had seemed to be a nice person. Emily was very defensive and felt that her daughter was being unusually harsh on her new man friend. In the face of this opposition from the younger generation, she married Perry. Then the troubles began.

All along Emily had been aware that Perry was an alcoholic, but she felt, as she had in her earlier marriage, that she could cure him. Of course that did not happen. To make matters worse, he was an extremely jealous, possessive man who watched every move that his wife made. If she so much lifted her head to look at a man, he would immediately suspect she was going to sleep with him and he would take her home and harass her about her interest in men. One day she went out with her son-in-law to get some groceries and when she returned he was standing suspiciously outside their house and immediately accused her of having an affair with him. This really shocked her. Perry would also frequently come home drunk and demand "to have sex with me." Of course she did not like having sex, but he would attempt to force himself on her. "It's dirty, its only for men," she complained. Why then did she remarry? "The soothsayer predicted."

Oftentimes the nuances of the parasexual and sexual aspects of marriage mirror the total relationship of the couple. The same power struggles and defense mechanisms, the same ability to be close or distant, the same spoiling of one's own or one's partner's pleasure at the moment of fulfillment, the same demands, the same masochistic or sadistic stance, the same dependent, childlike, or parental attitudes may prevail in sex as in other areas of the relationship (Sager, 1976). At other times, sex may appear as a unique parameter of couple interaction in which either spouse or both may act differently than in other areas of their lives. There are couples who fight, disagree on most values, and have constant power struggles, but continue to have an intense attraction for each other and are able to enjoy and fulfill each other sexually (Sager, 1976). In Emily's case it appeared as if they had a power struggle everywhere, in the kitchen as well as in the bedroom. Emily also appeared to use sex to get what she wanted, on her own terms. Though there appeared to be a sexual attraction between Emily and her new husband, there was complete denial of such feelings and the only reason given for being in this marital situation was the soothsayer's prediction.

It was quickly apparent that this marriage would not work. Perry was severely diabetic, but had not mentioned this before they were married. When Emily found out that she had a sick man on her hands, she resented it. She felt she had been deceived into marrying him. He needed extensive medical attention. She was extremely unhappy when she found out that he had to undergo an operation for gangrene. He did undergo this operation and his leg was amputated. He was "stuck" to a wheelchair and wanted Emily to push him around or stay close to him. Emily herself had had one kidney removed. If she protested that she could not push him around in the wheelchair, he would get mad and tell her that she was "as strong as a horse" and a little pushing would not hurt her. This style of life started one year after they were married and with it was the harassment of being a woman without a "real" husband. A different family dance.

Four years passed. Emily was ready to die of exhaustion and anger. Her daughters and the sister of her first husband were very sympathetic and understanding and because of them she was able to sustain this difficult life. The marriage had a justifying and validating function—it kept the women together. Women family members were loyal to each other and this was related to alignments. This family also had a hidden agenda which said that women had to marry men who had defects that would cause the family sufficient problems to help the women regroup themselves. Thus, men were the scapegoats and played their roles very well because they were already designated for these roles before marriage.

After five years of an extremely unhappy life, as Emily put it, her husband died. Emily looked at me and sighed, "I was happy to see him go. He was a problem, and a troublemaker and it was such a relief." By this time she was in her sixties. She saw this husband die in bed as she had her first husband. He was attempting to get some sleep after the doctors had pronounced his situation as bad. She took her Bible and read it and at the same time she was worrying about his will, because it was in his first wife's name and he owned a small store in the neighborhood. So, the lawyer was called in, the appropriate questions were asked and answered, and then Perry signed the will, leaving whatever he had for Emily. Emily added sarcastically, "It was not much, it just paid for his funeral." When his own daughter heard of the change in the will, she confronted Emily about it, saying that the money should go to her. However nothing came out of this and Emily used the money to bury him. All that was left of that marriage were ill feelings between herself and the daughter.

After this, she did not go to the soothsayer; she did not wish to know if she would remarry. She smiled and said, "After Perry and his crazy ways," she had decided to "give up on marriage" for a while and then decided it was not for her, permanently.

DEVELOPMENTAL FRAMEWORK IN THE THIRD GENERATION

Emily's older daughter, Joan, was doing better than her younger daughter, Colleen. She therefore decided to move in with Joan, who would be able to take good care of her.

What kind of life did the daughters lead? From the time they were young they learned not to trust or like men, because the family myth said that men were bad and could not be trusted. Also, they hardly knew their father. Their contact with him was minimal. As there were constant quarrels in the family, he would go away to keep peace or come home late at night after the children were asleep. On the other hand, there was a very closely-knit alliance between mother and daughters, as well as with the sister-in-law who lived next door. Strangely enough, the family always came up with more female children than male children. This was true of Emily's mother's family, Emily's family and, as we will see, Emily's daughters' families.

Joan, the older daughter, did not have any children. Though she did not like sex (Emily winced), Joan, according to her mother, hoped that she would become pregnant but this did not happen. When she was in her thirties, she and her husband adopted a girl, Christina. Christina grew up beautiful but defiant.

Emily's younger daughter, Colleen, was more of a daughter after her mother's heart—she did not like sex but did the right thing (as it was considered in those days) and got married. Her husband, William, was also a drunkard, but "not as bad as Joan's husband." Colleen, unlike her sister, Joan, would complain to her mother about how she despised sex and how it made her sick. The mother was aware of everything that happened in her daughters' lives. As Komarovsky (1964) recorded, some women go along with everything the mother tells them, constantly seeking her advice; the mother is usually the kind of person who would run their life if allowed to do so.

Despite her feelings about sex, Colleen gave birth to a daughter, Lucy, and then became ill. She suffered from a number of allergies and was constantly indisposed and unavailable to her husband; thus, the husband had to cater to her because she was such a weak person. He could not afford to be without a job nor could he drink too much because his wife needed him. For the past 25 years, Colleen has been in bed much of the time. "Poor thing, she is so weak," said Emily. I wondered about that; it was a powerful way of controlling a family, to have minor complaints and have other family members catering to the "sick person" all the time. Thus, in many ways Colleen controlled her marriage relationship as well as the family situation through her aches, rashes, sniffles, colds, and so forth. How could two people be irresponsible in a family? One had to give in and take care of the other and the husband was chosen for this role; thus, problems in this family revolved around Colleen's ill health.

To Colleen, Lucy was a fine and beautiful girl, unlike her sister's daughter, Christina, who according to Emily was, after all, adopted and did not know how to behave as a member of the household. When asked to elaborate, Emily mentioned that Christina was defiant towards her mother and her grandmother and said that she did not belong to them as she was adopted and therefore would not listen to them. Emily grumbled, "Adopted children are not really your children and they will never feel the same about you as a child that is born out of you." This was constantly thrown at Christina and "rightly so," Emily added. Christina had a bad mouth and would tell her mother off, frequently and angrily.

Life as a Member of Joan's Household

Emily went to live with her older daughter, Joan. She now trusted Joan's judgement because she had advised the mother not to marry her second husband. Thus, the symbiosis between mother and daughter created an intensely gratifying mode of relatedness that allowed each participant to luxuriate in feelings of infantile satisfaction as well as in omnipotent mother fantasies

(Bowen, 1978). Despite its torment, this afforded precious gratifications. Bowen approaches symbiosis from the undifferentiated ego mass perspective. He views it as a fused cluster of egos that are more completely fused into a mass than others. Certain egos are intensely involved in the family mass during emotional stress and are relatively detached at other times (Bowen, 1978).

Emily started to talk about her life with her older daughter. They lived in an apartment on the first floor. Emily thought a bit and commented that she had never seen so much anger and strife. Joan's husband was also a slightly suspicious man, but through the years Joan learned to tolerate this behavior. There were constant fights between Joan and her husband, Frank. Unlike Emily's husbands, Frank was a wife abuser and child beater. One day, he came home late and demanded that his wife cater to him. There was a lot of yelling, screaming and crying. At this point the teenaged daughter took a curtain rod and threw it at her father. He jumped on her and beat her up. While he was doing this, Joan stepped in to rescue her daughter, but he was completely out of control and would not let go of the daughter. Joan hit him and he then turned around and started to beat her.

Emily was frightened and angry. She ran to the rescue of her daughter, asking Frank not to beat her, but he did not listen. When she interfered, he pushed her around and also hit her once. Emily was shocked when he added, "You, old woman, it's bad enough I have to take care of you, go sit in a corner and don't interfere in my family life." This was the most painful thing that Emily had ever heard in her life. She was humiliated and horrified. This was only the beginning. Later on, he would scold her and shove her around physically if she was in his way; she hated him. She tried to persuade her daughter to divorce him, but her daughter insisted that Catholics do not divorce.

Emily was crying as she told this and my heart went out to her. She related the following incident. One day, her daughter and her husband were having a bad fight. Joan ran to the mother, complaining about him. Even before Emily could open her mouth, he was standing right close to her, close enough to knock her down, and told her that he would "kill her" if she interfered in his life. Then without any provocation, he slapped her hard in her face, at least three or four times. How did her daughter react to this? Joan was scandalized and upset but also helpless. Emily desperately urged her daughter to divorce him, which she did, some months after Emily started to live with them. In spite of their Catholic teachings, Emily felt that God would not punish them if they (she and her daughter) got rid of a man who was cruel and did not respect anyone. The power of the mother-daughter relationship was vivid; Joan had been married to her husband for over 30 years. The period of time she lived with her daughter was, for Emily, the most miserable part of her life.

One day Emily was walking down the stairs when she suddenly felt faint. A shooting pain went through her arms and she felt her left arm go limp. She was rushed to a hospital and was told that she had just had a stroke. Emily felt she needed her daughters and her sister-in-law around her. However, Margaret, her sister-in-law, did not come and a few months later Emily learned that her favorite sister-in-law had had a heart attack and died in Florida. Emily stayed in the hospital for some time, had a second stroke and lost the use of one of her legs. Then her ''bladder gave way'' and she was fitted with a bag to hold the urine. With all these medical problems, Emily could not be taken care of in the family, so she was placed in this agency for more appropriate care.

In the Life of Her Granddaughters

How were her granddaughters doing? Her second daughter's daughter, Lucy, was married. Naturally, her husband, Peter, was no good. He was uncaring, drank a lot, and lived on welfare. He had not held a job in the past 13 years, except for occasional odd jobs, and was a peripheral figure in the family. They had one child, a daughter. Lucy spent most of her time taking care of her mother who was sickly.

Joan's adopted daughter, Christina, was living with a man and had his child. At this time the child was 14 months old, but Christina and her boyfriend, Jim, had no intention of getting married. Thus, this picture was also incomplete in Emily's mind. Unlike the other grandson-in-law, Jim was not a bum, though he did drink, too. Jim held seasonal jobs laying sidewalks and driveways and made fairly good money. Emily criticized Christina, saying if she were her real granddaughter she would not be living with a man without being married. She thought for a moment and commented, ''Adopted children are different and of course Christina was no different.'' She and her boyfriend quarreled a lot and would get into physical fights. Christina would go home to stay with her mother for short periods of time before he would come to fetch her back.

ROLES OF MEN AND WOMEN IN THIS FAMILY

Women in this family, it appeared, almost went out of their way to choose men who would discredit themselves. Men were the stigmatized scapegoats. It appears that there is a marital collusion between husband and wife about the roles they can play. There is also the process of secondary identification which is a reciprocal process for the children who carry it over into their own marital relationships. Scapegoats are important because everything painful and evil and difficult could be placed on them and they would be labeled as evil people.

Though the women formed a close-knit group, when it came to marriage they chose men who would become their own personal scapegoats. This would draw the women even closer together as they continued to treat men as outsiders. What is the stigma borne by these men? When a person is labeled as weak, dangerous or bad, this person is reduced from a whole person worthy of respect to a tainted discounted one. The term stigma is used to refer to an attribute that is deeply discrediting. As the Greeks used it, stigma referred to bodily signs that exposed something unusual about a person as well as some information about the moral status of the signifier. Like ex-mental patients, alcoholics must face the prejudice against them as well as the disillusionment of those who expect to change them magically (Goffman, 1963). Historically, Emily's father was an alcoholic, as were Emily's husbands, her daughters' husbands and her granddaughters' spouse and cohabitor. This tells something about the place of alcoholism in this family. Men are married with the notion that they could be changed. When this does not happen, the negative, prejudiced attitudes about these men and all men are confirmed.

The women in this family, through hidden as well as verbal communication, share with each other the common problems of living with an alcoholic. To protect themselves against their poor marital relationships, the women create a network for themselves. These women are in constant crisis and the network protects them from their own men.

Networks consist of people and relationships. Bott (1957) uses the concept of social networks in her study of working-class London families. Her discovery that the networks of a marital couple affect the nature of their relationship with each other added an important dimension to the concept. This concept is incorporated in Mitchell's definition of a network, as a specific set of linkages which as a whole may be used to interpret the social behavior of the persons involved (Bott, 1957).

Networks can be personal as well as general. In this particular context, we are dealing with personal networks that include people who are connected through intermediaries or directly with a central figure or another person; in this family, it was a matriarchical figure, a mother, a grandmother, and so forth.

Craven and Wellman (1973) describe three aspects of networks that are theoretically useful: (1) density, (2) range, and (3) pathways. Density can be expressed in the ratio of actual links in the network to potential ones. A range refers to the number of individuals involved in the network, and a path refers to the direct or indirect link that exists between one individual and another through an intermediary or, as seen in this family, directly, without an intermediary. This family can be described as having a relatively dense network of limited range, with strong linkages among the family members. The world of men was separated from the world of women. The women were close, with similar interests as well as attitudes. As Emily initially mentioned, "Men are different, they do not feel the same way we do."

The parental family appeared to be the major source of socialization for this family. As Komarovsky (1964) put it neatly, though much has been written about the wide gap between generations allegedly so characteristic of rapidly changing societies, the impressive fact about Glenton (a working-class town) was the narrow generational cleavage. The parental family within which the men and women lived was the place where they acquired their conception of marriage roles and that remained their major reference group after marriage. The mother, for example, may be considered to be old-fashioned about sex and religion in most respects. Yet the married woman's guide was still her mother and certainly not a marriage manual or even her own peer group.

This seemed true in Emily's household as well. Moreover, there appeared little separation and individuation between the mother and her daughters. The term separation signifies the intrapsychic developmental track of differentiation, distancing, boundary formation, and disengagement from mother. Individuation denotes the evolution of intrapsychic autonomy—that is, the development of psychic structure and personality characteristics. How does this development take place in a person? As Edward, Ruskin and Turrini (1981) put it, children move from autism, to symbiosis, through four subphases of separation-individuation—differentiation, practicing, rapprochement and a fourth open-ended subphase. From here, the child advances toward a position of object constancy. However, this opportunity was absent in the Crosby household. The loyalty among these women is tight, their relationship with their fathers negative and superficial. The child remains in a symbiotic obligation bond with the mother. The loyalty-trapped child owes the parent her symptom, which in this case is choosing an alcoholic husband. She does not bring about any changes in her own life-style, which appears to be replicating her mother's.

Finally, there is no mixing with outsiders. This is a close-knit group where dependency needs are expressed only through female members. In such a relationship, an incapacity for repaying carries with it an arrest of receiving on the part of the child. A seeming antithesis of receiving through giving resolves itself in the dialectics of normal parenting. The parent gives to the child, but implicitly expects repayment, and the child receives but hopes someday to return benefits not only by actual day-to-day exchanges of their relationship, but by the entire family network of obligations.

POSTSCRIPT

I went back to see Emily after a gap of a year and a half. She was in good health, though she was confined to bed more often. She used her wheelchair to take her to the recreation and dining rooms; otherwise, she felt better in bed. She had undergone two more urinary tract operations. She shared pictures of her great grandchildren and at 81 years of age, her memory was remarkably accurate when she repeated some of the incidents that we had discussed in my earlier interviews with her.

She looked queenly as she lay on her bed, and when I was leaving, I commented, "You look beautiful." "Nah," she responded, "Life is bad! See how I have to be in bed . . . almost all the time." Emily saw negatives, I thought to myself, far better than positives.

CHAPTER 4

In the Life of Paul Fink

A beautiful nine-and-one-half-pound baby boy, with large blue eyes and no hair, was wheeled out of the delivery room. His father, Charles, ran anxiously to greet his newborn, long awaited son; his wife had been in difficult labor for over a day and a half. He looked at his son, smiled, had a heart attack, and died. Thus, Paul was born, the youngest of six children, the mother's pet and the envy of his brothers. His only sister doted on him as if he were her own child. In this way began the family dance in the Paul Fink family.

Dancing, of course, is a muscular exercise that calls for smoothly coordinated movement. In order to acquire this skill, dancers have to practice sufficiently so that the muscles perform with ease and grace. Until people have mastered the step patterns and can concentrate on the rhythm of the music, none of the dancers would enjoy performing it. It is the same with families: How well members fit in depends upon the manner in which they have learned the rhythms and steps of the family dance.

Paul at 70 years of age looked regal with silver hair and smoky blue eyes. His oversized nose appeared to dominate his face. When he put out his hand to greet me, I found that I was shaking the palm; the fingers were stubs. My eyes traveled to his legs

FAMILY TREE OF PAUL FINK

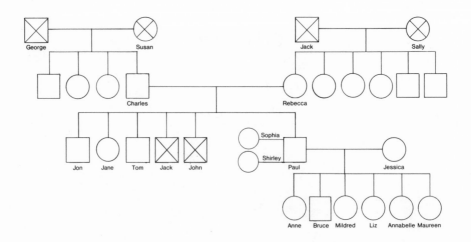

and instead of feet, he had blunt stubs. I wondered what had happened but did not pursue the topic. I felt that he would talk about it while taking me through his life course.

EARLY CHILDHOOD

With the birth of Paul, the life-style of the family changed. His mother, Rebecca, became a widow and had to take care of the family needs, financial and otherwise. The children in the family who were used to a different type of slow dance had to readjust themselves to a more hectic style. They had to pitch in, whenever possible, in doing housework, as well as in bringing home money from odd jobs. The father, Charles, had been a good provider, a railroad worker who earned enough to satisfy their needs. Now Paul's mother worked as a cleaning woman in restaurants located on boats; she managed to bring home leftovers that provided them with good meals. In spite of hard times, the mother managed to put food on the table and saw that the children wore clean clothes.

Developmental Framework

Paul came from a German-English background. It appeared that his parents came from families where men were viewed as being psychologically weak and the women had to take care of them. Family members learned to deny the presence of strength in men. These denied aspects of self were carried over to the family of procreation where the rules of interaction specified: "Do not recognize that men have strengths." Thus, in Paul's parents' family there was a family myth that men were weak and had to be taken care of by women; if not they would die. Charles Fink's death reinforced this feeling strongly in the family.

Charles had one brother who died young and two sisters. His parents had married young, and even at that time Charles' father, George (Paul's grandfather), was in pain; he had broken his leg while in his teens and it continued to bother him. When George married Susan, she was still in her teens. He was often confined to home and his wife, with the help of her family and relatives, learned to take care and provide for this family. Thus, the family had a weak, dependent man. Long after his death, he was known to his grandchildren as the "crippled grandpa."

Paul began to talk comfortably about his mother Rebecca and her family. He mentioned that they came from "good stock." His mother had three sisters and two brothers. In this family, too, Rebecca's mother, Sally, had to take care of them because her husband, Jack, traveled from place to place in search of jobs and was also "a little weak about drinking." At times, when he did not come home, Sally would send her sons to look for him. She would feed him and put him to bed as if he were a child. As his wanderings away from home increased, Sally moved back to her relatives' home and the children were brought up without the father. The absent father would sporadically visit the family and eventually died a drunkard. It was strange but true that Paul Fink came from stock on both sides where women had to cater to men and men were viewed as "weak."

Paul's mother and his sister were overprotective of Paul as a "boy" child. It appeared that he was more precious to his mother because his father died when he was born. He was a replacement for her husband and had to be taken care of diligently. However, his brothers did not care too much for him and often teased and taunted him.

As a child Paul went to a Catholic school and studied up to eighth grade. He mentioned that he disliked school intensely because the nuns used to beat the children.

LIFE STRUCTURING

The concept of a life structure—the basic pattern or design of a person's life at a particular time—gives us a way of looking at the engagement of the individual in a social group. This concept provides a tool for analyzing what is called "the fabric of one's life." Through life structuring we will be able to see how the self is in the world and how the world exists in the self. The life structure is seen in these perspectives as the individual's sociocultural world, as some aspects of a person's life are lived out, and the person participates in the world at large (Levinson, 1978).

The life structuring in this family specified that family members had to be hardworking, particularly the women. The fact that Paul's birth caused the father enough tension to kill him was discussed time and again in this family, reinforcing the defensive and protective attitude of women towards men. Every time this was mentioned, Paul felt uneasy for he often sensed that he was being silently accused for his father's death. Thus, life patterns were being set up for Paul while he was growing up in this family. Rules of behavior, regulations about what was acceptable and what was not acceptable, taboos and rituals that were part of family behavior became a part of Paul's life structuring. This life structure could be modified and built as a person becomes more individuated, depending upon his or her needs and abilities. Just as dance was used by primitive people to convey their emotions as well as beliefs and to carry out rituals and ceremonies, family dances develop, metaphorically speaking, to give meaning to a person's life in terms of rituals, emotions and beliefs.

Family Roles and Role Structuring

Paul's early years were uneventful. He remembers spending a lot of time with his sister, Jane, and, at times, with his older brother, Jon. He vividly remembers that his brothers and his sister gave the mother complete respect and obedience. This appeared to hold the family together. As we were talking, one stray incident stood out in Paul's mind. He recalled when he fell and hurt his knee badly; his older brother carried him running all the way home. There was a belief in this family that, like his father, Paul was not a strong person. The main impressions that he carried from his childhood was that he was an overly-protected child.

Family members played different roles. The oldest daughter, Jane, was the parentified child. She took care of everyone and everything when the mother was working. She could not attend school because she was overburdened with the physical care of her siblings. Some children are unceasingly loyal and will assign themselves as physical and psychological guardians to one or both parents if they sense unmet needs. These are the parentified children and Jane was one of them.

What is role structuring? All of Paul's siblings had roles that they lived up to. When certain roles frequently appear in families, they also help to identify structural patterns. Role structuring is a significant aspect of family living and roles are assigned and assumed in the family, along with relationships among members. These roles, unlike work or social roles, are definitely more permanent, less flexible, and also used less consciously. Each of us is aware that there is a great deal of overlap between who we are in our families and what we feel is our identity. Trying to change roles in a family is often like trying to struggle out of a straitjacket (Karpel and Strauss, 1983). Roles organize who we believe we are and how we act, as well as how others feel they are and how they act towards us.

The development of roles within families is an extremely complex process which involves transactions between and among members, intrapsychic experiences within members, and multigenerational legacies. How does a family role get created? The process begins with one or more members who need someone to fill a role. A mother, for example, who wants to take care of an insecure, dependent infant could create such a person. Similarly, a father may need a parent figure to take care of him; a couple may need someone to blame for their own problems, etc. These people are likely to manipulate other people and many situations in order to have their needs met.

In families, one of the most powerful and common ways of influencing one another and assuming such roles involves "attributions" (Karpel and Strauss, 1983). Instead of telling someone what to do, the family, by common repetition, tells a person who he or she is. As seen in the Fink family, Jane is constantly reminded that she is the caretaker of the family and she fills that role. Paul is told that he is the "baby" in the family and he acts accordingly.

This does not mean that all roles are forced upon family members. One who accepts the role of a scapegoat is not just a helpless victim; this person may participate in these situations out of a sense of loyalty to other family members, understanding at some level that this type of sacrifice is necessary for the survival of the family (Karpel and Strauss, 1983). Thus, myths are created around these restricted roles. Even in the most negative roles, there are some specific rewards such as freedom to get into trouble and to ask for protection, along with a sense of importance, however negative this might appear to be. Another reason why members accept and act out roles is the sense of identity and belonging that goes along with these roles. A family member constantly gets into trouble because he or she would rather get negative attention from the family than no attention at all.

Roles are often assumed because one family member wants another member to take on a complementary role. In order for one person to assume one role, the other has to assume a reciprocal role. If one person acts as the "strong person," the other would have to function as the "weak person." A husband might appear good when his wife is bad. When these complementary roles are viewed together with a person's identity or self-image, we understand why family members resist attempts to change their own or another family member's role. People learn to live up to their roles because any change could be a threat to their own reciprocal roles and, in turn, to their sense of identity (Barnard and Corrales, 1979).

In the Fink family, the sons shared the parental role off and on, in terms of providing for the family. Otherwise they appeared to spend more time away from their family. In many ways Paul was the "baby" of the family. In Paul's own words, he was "babyfied." He was encouraged to be dependent and this probably affected his psychological growth. He felt that his two older brothers, Jack and John, scapegoated him, often blaming him for small problems in the house which made him unhappy and uncomfortable. However, he knew that if he complained, his sister would come to his rescue. He never really understood why he was the odd one left out by these older brothers. "You know, I was not really responsible for my father's death, but those fellows never liked me."

His two older brothers, Jack and John, were close to each other. They did things together and kept everyone else out of their secrets. When they were teenagers, they went to swim in Lake Erie and never returned. Their bodies were never found. This was another tragedy that struck the family. The mother became even more overprotective of Paul and his older brother Jon. It was during this tragic period that Paul left school and started to take up odd jobs, so that he could also provide for the family. All through his teen years he worked at odd jobs, such as sorting out garbage near the railroad to see if anything of value could be taken home.

His older sister, Jane, and his older brother, Jon, married but continued to be close to the mother. Family loyalty appeared to run high. There was a sense of obligation and entitlement. "Mother did so much for us that there is nothing we can do that would repay her," was the constant family theme. She had sacrificed for the sake of her children and they would do everything they could to make her life more comfortable. This obligation or entitlement was an endless process and it appeared to underlie their relationship with the mother.

Throughout the interviewing there was no mention of the sec-

ond brother, Tom. Whenever this topic came up, Paul would successfully change the subject. At last, in the third interview with
Paul, he spoke of his brother. It was dramatic. At first he wanted
the door to be closed and then the tape recorder shut off as he
was telling me, an outsider, a family secret. He mentioned that
this brother was a "queer," he did not date girls and he spent
all his time with men. This appeared to be a shared family secret
that involved all members of the family but was kept from outsiders. Tom's homosexuality was a family secret not discussed
among family members but subtly understood. In some ways this
strengthened the boundaries that separated the family as a whole
from the outside world. It is true in this case that the loyalty
dynamics maintained the secret in the family. Almost 40 years
later while disclosing the secret, Paul experienced a feeling of
betrayal that aroused guilt in him. He mentioned that this brother
was very handsome, with a moustache, but "He could also look
beautiful, like Rita Hayworth." He was a loner and did not have
much to do with the family.

It appeared that this secret strengthened alliances and boundaries among its holders. There was resentment in the family
towards Tom, particularly by the brothers, which led Tom to
withdraw from family interactions and become a loner. At an
emotional level, this created anxieties for family members as this
secret continued to be a taboo topic. Individual family members
and the family as a whole suffered the loss of relational resources
that results from secrets. Secrets interfere with person-to-person
relationships that are essential in differentiated and reciprocal-
ly balanced systems. Often, they contribute to the formation of
pseudobonds instead of genuine alliances; when stresses arise,
they could lead to unnecessary estrangements (Boszormenyi-
Nagy and Spark, 1973).

This happened in Paul's home; it appeared that there was a
collusion against Tom where two of his brothers, Jack and John,
kept away from him. Neighbors often asked why Tom did not
date and they would explain that he was busy working. When
Tom was in his twenties, it was an embarrassment to the family
that he spent all his time with men. However, this was not

discussed in the family. At times, for no apparent reason, there would be serious fights between the brothers and one of them would get violent with Tom. Paul was too young to participate and at that time was not really sure of the reasons for the fights. Later in his life he suspected that Tom's sexual orientation could have been a reason for this type of fighting.

Quarrels

On analysis it could be said that quarrels are more likely to start when two family members do not trust each other, when the life situation of one causes embarrassment to the other, and when they cannot treat each other as equals. Quarrels could also occur when some members of the family try to dominate others. The fact that Tom's homosexual life-style was a taboo topic in the family could have spurred quarrels by family members who felt that they were different from Tom. Yet they constantly protected him from the outside world and from each other. When the brothers fought over trivia, it was because they were always alert for clues that would release their pent-up feelings. Paul did not get into fights with Tom because he was so much younger. However, when Paul "figured him out," he felt extremely resentful. It appeared to the men in the family that their masculinity was challenged by Tom's different sexual preference.

Paul confessed that he secretly blamed this brother when there were misunderstandings and quarrels in the family. However, he did not directly attack his older brother. He showed his resentment toward him by coldness and sullenness. At last, one day, when he could no longer take his brother's "peculiar" sexual preference, Paul was surprised by his own burst of anger and temper, triggered by a petty incident. Often Tom was blamed for problems for which he was not responsible. For instance, one time when the older brother lost his job, Tom became the focus for blame and accusation and this took the heat off other problems in the family. It appeared that Tom was the chief scapegoat of the family.

Paul found himself individuating and moving away from the family while he was still in his teens. He dated four girls before he finally chose his wife. She came from an Italian-English background and was a good Catholic. After a period of two years, he decided to marry her. His mother, though happy, had difficulty attempting to redefine their relationship, which included issues of autonomy, responsibility, and loosing control over her youngest son. In many ways Paul was still an adolescent, but he was working and giving most of his money to his mother. The issues of identity were difficult because he was the "baby" in the family. Having an older gay brother, according to him, did not help. His oldest brother, Jon, had married and moved out and there was really no role model for Paul. However, he survived and decided to leave home to get married. This was a difficult period for him, for his mother became ill quite often. However, this was never discussed, as she would come up with statements like, "I am fine, it is you who needs to take care of yourself."

Marriage

Paul's marriage ceremony was clouded by a sad incident. All the marriage preparations had been completed. His mother went out the day before and cut her rather lengthy hair as she wanted to look fashionable on her youngest son's wedding day. She cooked and cleaned the night before the wedding. The next morning, while preparing pies, she had a heart attack and died. Nobody informed Paul of his mother's death and he was married that afternoon; he wondered where his mother was and was told that she was tired and taking a nap. A day later he learned that his mother had died. It shocked him. He was upset that he had not been informed, but his sister and brother felt that since he was a MAN he would not be able to stand the shock. Paul felt that perhaps he was the ill omen for his parents. He remembered that his father had died when he was born and now his mother died on his wedding day. Though he was not personally responsible, and nobody blamed him for his mother's death, he continued to feel guilty for a long time.

When Paul was about 30 another tragedy struck his family. His brother, Tom, had moved out of the house and had gone to New York. The family was relieved to see him leave. However, they continued to use their cover-up and told each other that Tom had gone to New York because he could find a better job, though all that Tom performed was odd jobs. After moving to New York, Tom reduced his communication with the family and nobody seemed to care. The only person with whom he was really in touch was his sister who, like her mother, felt that men were weak and had to be taken care of by women.

One day the family got the news that Tom had been involved in a bar brawl and was stabbed to death by another man. The details were still taboo and Paul had difficulty relating the incident, just vaguely mentioning that Tom was killed in a brawl. The family did not claim his body and there was no funeral for him. It was best that he be forgotten. Paul let out a long sigh . . . the family no longer needed to be protected. They had experienced so much stress with Tom that it was alright that he had to go the way he did. It was sad, of course, but without a funeral there was no need to offer explanations to relatives or neighbors; it was a family secret buried in guilt.

It appeared that there was a tight interlocking among the rest of the family members against this single family member. While completing the telling of this incident about his brother, Paul sighed again. He was uncomfortable because Tom had disappeared from the family scene and was never discussed. Paul seemed to be caught between loyalty and betrayal, fairness and unfairness, obligation and entitlement in this family relationship. He added that he was glad he was able to talk about it. Tom was never discussed in the family after his death. He was viewed as a weak man who had to be taken care of and when he left the protection of the family, without his sister who took an active interest in him, he was lost. Without his family's support he could not survive. Thus, Tom lived up to this particular family myth which said that men needed to be taken care of.

ADULTHOOD AND MIDDLE AGE

Paul moved out with Jessica, his wife, into a new apartment. He moved from odd jobs to a position as an interior decorator, making use of what he had learned in night courses. His income and family size increased. Like his parents he fathered six children, five daughters and a son. He enjoyed his children and was the chief disciplinarian. His wife was a timid person and a good housewife who took care of the children, cooking, and cleaning. Of course, the daughters pitched in. His only son was exempt from housework because he was more "delicate" and needed to be taken care of. Developmentally this appeared to be a couple myth by the process of marital collusion. There was splitting and denial of strength in men; there was the presentation of the false self in this family and this was carried over and later became a cross-generational myth as well.

Jessica and Paul made a compatible pair because they both came from families that believed in the innate weaknesses of men. Jessica came from a family of five children, four daughters and a son. The son was pampered and taken care of in a protective fashion. Her father was Italian and a gang member, but at home he was "nurtured" by his wife and daughters. In many ways this appeared to provide the protective function of holding the family together.

Tragedy also struck Jessica's parents when her father was killed by his gang for talking too much. There was shared denial on the part of the family that the father had done anything wrong. His death was attributed to the fact that he was a weak person and always needed his wife; without her at his side, he went astray. This was obviously an implausible, defensive explanation, but one that held the family together.

Let us go back to Paul's life and the pathways that myths took in his life. All the children in Paul's family had roles that they lived up to.

Paul described his oldest daughter as irreplaceable; there was no one like her in the family, she was indispensable, and she lived up to that description. She helped his wife with housework and was always there with a smile to receive her father when he came home. She could run the house better than anyone else and he was glad that he was blessed with such a child. Whenever his wife was indisposed, Anne would manage the house just as well as or even better than his wife. This daughter gave him more satisfaction as a child in her "complete housewife" behavior than any of his other children. It was a blessing because his wife needed a helper. With a satisfied smile, he added, "She is still the same, an extremely responsible mother and wife."

He described his second child and only son, Bruce, as a serious person. He added with an indulgent smile, "He's a boy, you know." I wondered what that meant, really. He did do outdoor work, but in the house he expected everything to be perfect from his food to the manner in which his clothes were folded. Everyone in the family gave in to him as he was the only brother for his five sisters as well as an only son to his parents. When it was cold, or rained too much, it affected Bruce and he was given a lot of caring. Bruce was extremely task-oriented but needed his mom for advice and help. I had a feeling that we were up against myths once again. Men need to be pampered in this family. The parents appeared to be protective towards Bruce who, in turn, remained totally loyal to the family by acting out the role that was prescribed for him.

Paul described his second daughter, Mildred, as vain, and selfish, unlike the other members of the family. She would want money for her clothes and makeup and didn't care if other members of the family got nothing. Her chief interest was herself; she hardly helped in any housework and whiled away her time singing with the radio and meeting friends. The father was aware that she would not amount to anything "and she did not," he added. She married a man without much money and still spends more of her time on herself than on her children or husband. They are constantly in debt. Well, her father did not "expect anything better from her." While growing up she was a complainer who spent her time finding fault about not having enough of something or the other. He frowned, "She was too much to handle." Had she changed as she grew older? Paul shook his head negatively. "No, she is still the same, always complaining." She rarely visits him and when she does, she does not leave without complaining about something or other. It appeared that this was the "bad child" of the family and she had retained this role to fulfill family needs as well as self needs; in the process she helped maintain the coherence of the family.

Paul smiled when he thought of his third daughter, Elizabeth. "She was a pest," he said and that is how she was addressed in the family. She was lovely to look at, but was always teasing someone in the family. Nothing could upset her and even at the most difficult of times, she would be smiling or indulging in harmless teasing. She was nicknamed "pest" because that is the way she was. At times she would behave like a clown, but she could aggravate her siblings by her continual teasing. Did this child feel an obligation to be the clown and tease in the family? Was she the standard-bearer for the "light side of the family"? To what degree did she contribute to maintaining the coherence of the family? How was she at this point in her life? He smiled sadly and remarked "that she was a pest" until she died of cancer a few years ago.

The fourth daughter, Annabelle, was described as a "good" child. She listened to her mother and did whatever household chores had to be done. She was patient and kind like his wife. She would readily give up rewards for the sake of other siblings. She was a frail, considerate child and has continued to function in this manner.

The youngest child, Maureen, was the best of the lot, he added with a smile. She was the "queen" of the family. She was beautiful to look at, could sing like a bird, and was dainty and delicate. In this family everyone catered to her because she was the youngest as well as the prettiest. She was, of course, the pampered child in the family. Everyone liked her, it was impossible not to. "She was a special child and had continued to be so," he added. She married a well-to-do man and they own grocery stores. Everyone in the family was proud of her. However, Paul was not surprised that she had made out so well. After all, she was the "queen" and one would not expect her to do otherwise.

It appeared that all the children in the family had been nick-named with their role and each child's behavior reflected the myths that were created in this family. Myths of harmony as well as myths of catastrophe were present and somehow they helped to maintain the coherence of the family. I wondered how one child in a family could be all good and another all bad, how they get selected for such roles, and what needs this selection satisfied in the parents, child, and other family members? Children de-velop an identity of self depending upon the powerful injunc-tions they receive at home. In Erikson's (1959) view, identity is a conviction that the ego is learning effective steps towards a tangible, collective future and is developing into a defined ego within a social reality. He describes it as a part of an individual's core which connects to the group's inner coherence. Identities are also retained because of the loyalty that the family members feel for and towards each other. As Boszormenyi-Nagy & Spark comment (1973), loyalties are the result of external expectations and internal obligations. In this family it appeared that at least two of the children were similar to the mother. The "irreplace-able" and the "good" child would carry on the mother's tradi-tion. They were legacy carriers, as was the son, for though he was serious-minded, he needed his mother to take care of him. Somehow this son carried the legacy of being the "weak child" or, better still, the weak son. Thus a cross-generational myth was already in bloom while this son was growing up.

Though Paul's wife was also frail and constantly needed help with housework, and there was another daughter who was sick-ly, this was not seen as significant. In this family, there was an atmosphere of harmony and individualized rules of behavior that viewed some children as positive and others as more negative. According to the family's rules, certain members could be criti-cized or challenged, but others had to be left alone. Roles had become fixed to suit this family's needs. Why some members were favored and others were not was, of course, beyond the realm of consciousness and reality.

Unconsciously, man adapts himself, his way of life, and his dances to the particular environment of which he is a part (Bentovim, Barnes, and Cooklin, 1982). In a similar manner, in families, members get enjoined to wear masks or assume roles that help towards maintenance of the family. Different family members cleverly retain their identity and self in this family situation.

OLDER YEARS

As time passed, Paul's six children grew up. When the youngest child was in her early adolescence it became apparent that the mother, Jessica, was suffering from cancer. However, this information was not shared with the entire family. Jessica felt that her husband was too weak to receive such information. She had breast cancer and after a visit to the doctor, she told her oldest daughter, Anne, about it. This was a secret between the two of them; not sharing it with the rest of the family created an alliance between mother and daughter. They felt they were protecting the family. However, the reality was that the women were just as weak as the men, but this was a taboo topic and could not be discussed. The mother's cancer was a family secret and was shared between two family members. This also led to the mother telling the father white lies in order to protect him. It created internal subgroupings within the family. As in the case of all secrets, there was confusion about it because the father suspected something was wrong but could not identify it.

How did two members of a family, a married daughter and her mother, maintain a secret? It is almost impossible to overemphasize the significance of loyalty dynamics in the creation, maintenance, and eventual facing of secrets in the family. In this case the daughter was sworn to silence by the mother; therefore, for the daughter to reveal the secret would be an act of betrayal. It would arouse guilt over the feeling of disloyalty. Such situations create split-level patterns where one person is loyal to one parent and disloyal to another, the rationalization in this situation being that the father would be too weak to accept the situation, though ironically it was the wife and mother who was dying. Of course Paul suspected that something was wrong, because he would often hear his wife and daughter discussing something, but the conversation would die out when he entered the room.

Slowly, the cancer took over; Jessica developed cancer in her second breast as well, and at this point Paul had to be told, as the cancer was spreading rapidly. In relating this, Paul fell silent for a long time. He sighed and mentioned that in those days they did not have good medications for cancer. How did he feel about it? He said he was angry with his daughter for not telling him. Though he loved this daughter very much and she was a source of support to him and his wife he could not forgive her for not telling him. He overlooked the fact that his wife also did not inform him. He added that he and his wife were a very happy couple, with tremendous togetherness, though this appeared to be in disparity with what had happened. I realized that I was being confronted with the myth of harmony.

I wondered about the daughter. Did she have guilt feelings about this incident or did she come to terms with it, viewing it from the mother's perspective. It appeared as if the daughter had been scapegoated in this particular incident.

Slowly, every member of the family came to know of the mother's cancer. This knowledge of her illness appeared to strengthen the boundaries in the family. The two older married children visited the mother frequently, while the rest of the children stayed home. Jessica became completely emaciated. She was pale and no longer cheerful or friendly. She was in a lot of pain and finally faded away, slowly but steadily.

After his wife's death, Paul became very depressed and the children felt that he needed them all the time. Often, Paul mentioned that he would kill himself and this frightened the children. One day, he took an overdose of sleeping pills. He did not die but it scared his children and from then on they spent more of their evening time with him than outside with friends. Did he really want to die at that time? He replied negatively. Every Saturday night the children would gather in the dining room and share a meal together. Even though some of the children would have preferred to go on dates, Paul proudly added, they stayed home for his sake. There was the presence of a less toxic myth in this family which said that all men in this family were weak; Paul was living up to the myth. By his attempting suicide, he kept the family completely together, almost unnaturally, with children staying home because their father could not bear to be alone.

Loss does have a terrible impact on the family. It is a powerful feeling, whether threatened, anticipated, denied, or actually experienced. The loss through death of a spouse or immediate family member such as a child or parent is one of the most stressful events we as human beings must face as this also means a major disruption in the organization of the family. Grieving such a loss is nature's way of attempting to heal the wound, as evidenced by the occurrence of mourning in all people (Bentovim, Barnes and Cooklin, 1982). Without his wife life was unbearable for Paul.

Stress

Stress reaches a state of imbalance when demand and the ability to cope are at variance. If normal coping is ineffective, stress is prolonged and abnormal responses occur. Such responses, may give rise to functional and structural damage. The progress of these events is subject to tremendous individual variation (Cox, 1978). All individuals experience and cope with stress. The degree of stress that a family member faces and the ability to cope with it depend upon the network of relationships of which one is a part.

The death of the mother was a powerful loss and had its impact on every member of the family. For a period of three years the children catered to the father, waiting for him to get remarried because men in this family needed women. There is evidence that when an older partner dies, there is increased incidence of mortality of the remaining partner in the first year of bereavement, estimated in studies to be 40 to 200 times as great as in the general population (Bentovim, Barnes and Cooklin, 1982). This did not occur in Paul's case, but there was an implicit cry for help by Paul through his suicide attempt. After this attempt there was an overprotective stance in which this fragile family member was protected by others. Paul's tales of the constant and frequent home gatherings gave a picture of a family where individual members clamored again to diffuse their boundaries and become a part of the parental subsystem, with protection as the chief aim and criterion.

Paul's Second Marriage

Paul met a beautiful woman, Sophia, who was a pianist, and he fell in love with her. According to Paul, his family was elated. They knew that he had a last found someone to take care of him, and within the next year the rest of his children got married. Paul did not think that this was unusual. His children had been dating and they just waited for him to find a mate before they launched their own marriages.

After a romantic courtship that lasted for six months, Paul married Sophia. She was beautiful to look at and came from a middle class family wealthier than he was. Their wedding took place in a church flooded with flowers from Sophia's two sons from her previous marriage. It was a beautiful wedding; later, her two sons presented them with foodstuffs that would last them a month.

Paul was extremely happy . . . but not for long. He soon found out that, besides music, his new wife liked other things like drinking and taking pills. He smiled sarcastically, "She was supposed to take care of me, but she did not." She was never sober. From early morning she drank on the sly. He caught her a few times and soon lost trust in her. The relationship between them was on the rocks within two months of the marriage. He could not believe that he had married such a person. Feelings of anger, guilt and shame overwhelmed him.

Feelings are inseparably connected to systemic and relational patterns, but they are experienced and expressed by individuals. Feelings of pride, shame, guilt, jealousy, and resentment in one individual can exercise a powerful influence on the structure and development of a relational system. Along with these feelings, Paul still hoped that his wife would listen to him and matters would change. However this did not happen, and he was filled with disappointment and discouragement. He attempted to control his wife by giving her an ultimatum that she must give up drinking and taking pills within a month.

Paul added that he was no saint. He did drink, but definitely not to the extent that his wife did. During this period he started to miss his first wife, Jessica, tremendously. He started to grieve profoundly. He experienced tremendous guilt and anger for marrying his second wife. This is technically called a morbid grief reaction. In a clinical study of 19 patients suffering from morbid grief (Lieberman, 1978), the signs and symptoms were evaluated using a Morbid Grief scale. The scale includes many of the most frequently observed reactions: absence of expected reaction, delayed reaction, avoidance, panic attacks, anniversary reactions, overidealization, identification symptoms, recurrent nightmares, extreme anger, extreme guilt, prolonged grief and physical illness (Lindemann, 1944; Parkes, 1972). It appeared as if Paul was still mourning for his first wife.

During this period Paul's second wife promised that she would not drink anymore. But that did not happen. One morning he was standing near a window where he could watch his wife when she went into the kitchen to get herself a cup of coffee soon after she got out of bed. He was surprised to note that instead of drinking coffee she poured herself a stiff drink of liquor and drank it down with a number of pills. Paul had had it. He walked to the bedroom, packed his bags and told her he was leaving for good. She looked at him, desperately. He left in spite of her protests and tearful promises that she would definitely give up drinking. He was simply tired of her lying.

Later that evening, while drinking in a bar, he realized that he had left one of his bags in his apartment, so he returned home. While he was climbing the steps the superintendent of the building came up to him and mentioned that there was no one upstairs. After a while the superintendent whispered that his wife had committed suicide by taking an overdose of pills. When she called the superintendent saying that she had drugged herself, they rushed her to the hospital where she died. Paul was heartbroken, but also filled with guilt that he had gotten involved with a woman who was beyond saving. In the few months that he had known her, he had not tried to find out anything about her background. He felt cheated by her and her sons. He had been handed a burden to carry and he could not do it. After all, he had married her hoping that she would take care of *him*. He was extremely unhappy, her face haunted him, her final plea, and the look in her eyes stayed with him for a long time. At times he could not sleep or he would wake up shivering and trembling, remembering this wife who was dead but was on his mind all the time. The memories were not pleasant and they haunted him.

During the following winter, Paul decided he could not stand it anymore. He also had been drinking a lot but he did not take pills. One evening, he took a "stiff" drink and wearing nothing but a pair of flimsy summer shorts and a shirt, he walked into a snowstorm that had just started; he walked for miles until he could walk no more. Finally, exhausted, he fell to the ground outside a church. Some priests saw him and carried him to a hospital. He survived, but was delirious for days. His nose, his toes, and part of his feet and fingers were frostbitten; toes and fingers had to be amputated, as well as one foot. His nose was swollen abnormally and no treatment would return it to normal size.

Paul underwent extensive treatment for a number of months. He recovered, but life had changed. He felt different about himself and about life itself. His children were furious that he had done this to himself deliberately. Only his youngest daughter, the "queen," felt sorry for him and told him that she understood what he felt. Moreover, she was the wealthiest of all his children and provided him with money and clothing. However, none of the children wanted to take him in permanently. He added that he did not want to bother them. That was how he became a resident of this agency.

Another tragedy struck this family. His daughter, Elizabeth, died of cancer. She suffered greatly, but only for a short period of time. However, the rest of his children worried that there was no woman to take care of their father. His youngest daughter would visit him often and question him closely about his life, especially about whether he was interested in anyone. His children and grandchildren appeared to gather around him on every occasion. To me as a researcher and outsider it was amazing how an almost similar scene had developed when the father was widowed the first time. Though the family worried about the weakness of men, it was amazing that he not only outlived his wives but had the stamina to walk through a blizzard in his mid-sixties and survive it. Though women had died of illness in the family—his first wife and one of his daughters—and his second wife had been a "weak" person who committed suicide, there was no discussion of women needing men.

Paul felt weak without a woman. He added, "There was no one to take care of me." His adult children constantly were on the lookout to see that he did not hurt himself. They continued to cater to him. Loyalty and feelings of guilt seemed to play a role in their lives. It was Maureen, the youngest daughter, who catered to the father more than the others. There were a number of reasons for this. She was his favorite daughter, and more prosperous than her brother and sisters. Moreover, as the youngest child in the family, this "adult child" was in a "binding mode" with her father and was still a part of his life. Such children do not leave home psychologically; they often remain at home out of a mixture of concern for and attachment to the family, in this case to the father. This "delegated child" is sent out of the family with some kind of a mission to accomplish; they are held responsible, often covertly, by themselves and the family to pursue missions that are called for by the family structure and history. The adult children have to balance their loyalties and obligations to their family of origin while being aware of their obligations to themselves. Thus, a pattern of dual commitment arises, based upon the life-style of the family and the family themes that are followed.

In this family, a process developed where the responsibility and reciprocity between the parent and child changed. When they were young and the natural mother was living, the children had a relationship with the parents that was more unilateral in terms of caring and responsibility. This did not become a two-way street as happens when debts, legacies and loyalties have been worked through meaningfully between parents and children. Particularly after the mother died, it became lopsided and imbalanced, with the children catering to the father. Thus, once again the equation was completely imbalanced but, in terms of this family's lifestyle and myths, it was meaningful because there was a less toxic myth in the family that said men needed women to survive. With four living daughters, this myth worked out well for the father, Paul. His favorite daughter, the youngest adult child, and the rest of his children kept looking out for a person whom he might still marry.

Paul and Shirley

At last it happened, right in the agency. Paul was going to lunch in the dining room one day when he saw a lovely woman dressed in pretty clothes trying to get a tray for her food. He liked her at first sight and decided even before he had spoken to her that he would marry her. Later, he felt extremely happy when she was brought to his table for lunch. He introduced himself and found out her name was Shirley. He tried to talk to her but was surprised at her childlike innocence and ignorance of the world. She did not know how to read or write and could hardly speak. She had been misdiagnosed as retarded when she developed poor speech, but she was not really retarded. According to Paul, her childhood had been terrible. She was an adopted child and her parents did not really care for her. When they found that she could not communicate well, they stopped sending her to school. Instead of being an adopted daughter, she became an adopted maid who had to take care of her parents. This was because another child was born to them soon after Shirley reached her third year. Though her parents constantly said that they loved her, the treatment that she received at their hands was painful. They constantly talked of how different or stupid she was; in time this became true. She did feel stupid and did not acquire any skills, except those of a housemaid.

Now Shirley found a good friend in Paul and related her sad life history. Her parents had died when she was in her fifties and

Shirley was left penniless, though her sister was better off. Without money or shelter and unable to read or write, Shirley moved
from house to house as a housemaid for a few months until some
caring person referred her to this agency. Thus, she was admitted to this home primarily for social rather than medical reasons.
Paul was sympathetic to her and after a few months decided to
marry her. His children attended the wedding, which took place
in the agency. This time he felt that he had made the right choice.
She was charming and feminine, and would be able to take care
of him. In fact, right in the agency she took over all the work in
their room, making their beds, growing plants and doing cleaning. She even collected pictures, framing them or pasting them
on the walls. Indeed, Paul was a happy man at last. His children
gave a sigh of relief. Paul had settled down with someone who
would nurture him. He has been married to Shirley for the past
four years.

   As I sat with Paul for many hours discussing his life and the
routes it took, it became obvious that families are very powerful. They can force individuals into roles and create myths that
would hold them together or keep them apart, depending upon
the needs of a particular family. The myth that men were weak
was a powerful one in this family, though time and again women
collapsed and died. The family stayed with the myth that held
them together. "Men need women" was the myth that created
the much-needed harmony in the family. This appeared to be
true in Paul's family of origin and it was carried over to his family
of procreation. When Paul's first wife was sick, there was no communication between them about the illness. There appeared to
be pseudomutuality under the guise of protecting men; things
that were not discussed could be conveniently pushed under the
rug as "something men cannot take." Looking at Paul's life, one
can see that he was a survivor who got what he wanted. He was
taken care of by women though they appeared to be weaker than
he was. For example, while he criticized the parents of his new
wife for not caring for their daughter, in essence he treated her
the same for she catered to his every need; she waited on him
literally hand and foot. While I spoke with Paul, Shirley would

sit close by and he would ask her to get things for him—a towel, a tissue paper, a cigarette—or to push his wheelchair (though he could do it on his own), and so forth. It was a pattern that had been set. He needed her to take care of him and she did it. She whispered to me, "He needs me." They were a compatible pair and blended in neatly with Paul's family dance.

POSTSCRIPT

I went back to see Paul a year and a half later and we met several times, reliving his life and the myths that were a part of his life. It was encouraging to know that Paul's memory was still good. He was happy to see me and got more personal this time. During the second session, Shirley had gone down to get her hair done, and Paul got restless. "Remember what I told you, I need her." Then, with a twinkle in his eyes, this 71-year-old man said, "I need women." He certainly did; after an hour he got so restless that I asked him to find his wife and return; I felt myself being inducted into his family myths as I sensed and experienced their power.

CHAPTER 5

In the Life of Melissa Simpson

There was something serene and beautiful about Melissa. Her silvery, wavy hair and deep brown eyes added to her beauty. Melissa was born in Scotland but came to the United States with her family when she was less than three years of age. They lived in Pennsylvania most of her childhood years. Melissa was one of the children born to her parents, Oliver and Clara. A brother, Leonard, was six years older and a sister, Matilda, was eight years older than she. Six children had died during childhood.

FAMILY OF ORIGIN

The Mother

Melissa's mother, Clara, was a sickly woman with a bad heart. She continued to have children until her ninth child was stillborn. According to Melissa, her mother had at least 19 heart attacks or pains resembling heart attacks. She was taken to the hospital but was cared for at home. Melissa described her mother as being sickly and dependent upon other family members, but always "smiling." The emphasis on one member being sick addresses the family through its weaknesses, supporting a multidirectional dialogue of action and concern which capitalizes on the family's

FAMILY TREE OF MELISSA SIMPSON

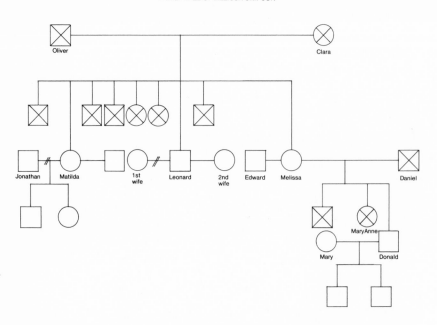

strength and resources (Karpel and Strauss, 1983). This appeared
to be true in Clara's case. The most vivid picture of her mother
that Melissa recalls is of a woman who was almost always in bed.
She was too weak to do housework and the children pitched in.

What were some of the outstanding impressions of her mother?
Melissa remembered her mother as sitting in her chair or lying
on her bed; she hardly ever walked. She always had a beautiful
smile on her face even though she was in pain. She never raised
her voice, was always gentle and quiet. She had a number of
Scottish friends who visited her frequently and with whom she
drank tea brewed from tea leaves. According to Melissa, all Scottish people drink tea. In those days, Melissa added, they did not
have teabags. When the tea leaves made a formation in the tea-
cup, her mother predicted a person's future by "reading" them;
people liked to go to her for this purpose and her mother was
always gentle in making positive predictions about the future.

But of course Clara would tire easily and Melissa's sister had to make sure that the friends left. Melissa remembers being interested in the facial expressions of these people who would take delight and encouragement in her mother's advice. Her mother was the central figure in the family. She had a low, sweet voice and everyone listened to her. Her mother constantly emphasized that they were happy people because they belonged to a happy family.

The Father

Oliver was a quiet man, doing things for his wife whenever he was home. He was a coal miner and they had lived in Pittsburgh for a long time. Later, he worked for a steel company in another community in Western Pennsylvania. Around Pittsburgh they had a large number of aunts and uncles and cousins who had emigrated to the United States at the same time as her parents. She had early recollections of the extended family, but after they moved away from Pittsburgh and as they grew older, their contact with their relatives was reduced considerably.

There was a power structure in the family typical of many Scottish families. Oliver was the head of the family and Clara was second in line, then the children hierarchically according to age. However, her father was a benevolent man who did not exercise his power in a negative way; he did not control his wife or children. They were a happy family and there was "no need for anyone to control anyone else."

The Sister

Matilda, her sister, was like a mother figure in the family. As far back as Melissa could recollect, it was her sister who did all the housework, from cooking, cleaning, washing, and baking bread to scrubbing floors and washing windows. Matilda had started to work in this manner right from the time she was 11 years of age because her mother was usually indisposed. Although Melissa was not aware of it when she was young, she realized later in life that her sister had been unhappy because she had to do so much housework. "Her girlhood was affected by it and she did not have time for anything she wanted to do."

Matilda was a serious person. Even as a child, she had assumed adult responsibilities and was really the family manager upon whom the parents depended. Though she worked the hardest, Matilda's clothes were not as nice as Melissa's. Matilda took care of Melissa and was more like a parent to her than a sister. They never quarreled.

What choices do young children have but to conform to the unrealities of the parent? An individual family member has pressure of the most powerful kind exerted upon him or her to conform to the rules that maintain the system. Family persuasive techniques can be obvious ones, ranging all the way from threats of physical punishment to withdrawal of love. The most effective influences, as Boszormenyi-Nagy and Spark (1973) see it, include threats of love withdrawal, forceful yet subtle guilt provocation, and the parentification of the child: "How can you be rude to your mother?" "How can you hurt your mother's feelings?" Melissa's mother is suffering from a heart condition, but talks too much to her friends. Her daughter has to worry about her and send her friends away when it seems appropriate. Matilda is the "family manager." Zuk (1981) indicates that parents who have been deprived of their own parents through loss or separation may unconsciously seek this relationship with a child, particularly if the marital partner fails to gratify this need. The child is then transformed into a parent figure.

In this family, Matilda had been pushed into a parental role. This turned out to have a detrimental effect on her own personal development. When she needed to become a dependent child again and get what she had missed in earlier years, she was subjected to the most damaging form of rejection. Because of their deep emotional investment in each other, family members exert a silent but potent influence on each other. The parentified child faces intense pressures to take up and stay in the parental role.

The Brother

Melissa's brother, Leonard, was the fun child in the family. He seemed like a happy-go-lucky person who helped Matilda with household chores whenever he could. He was a good brother and taught Melissa to play baseball and other sports, for which she was grateful. For him, everything appeared to be a pleasant challenge, from helping parents to taking care of his younger sister. He was well loved because he was such a good person.

Melissa

Melissa described herself as the most loved child in the family. She felt she was not as goodlooking as her sister or her brother, both of whom had beautiful blonde hair and blue eyes and were extremely attractive. Her own hair was dark like her mother's and her eyes were brown like her grandmother's. She was nicknamed "Granny." Melissa felt that this was a compliment because her grandmother was greatly respected in their family as a good, bright, softspoken person whom everybody loved and listened to. From a young age she tried to live up to this image and felt honored to be called "Granny." Her grandmother was a great singer and a voracious reader, with hands that were always busy knitting. Melissa resembled her grandmother physically, developed a good singing voice, and saw herself as the "pet" in the family.

During Christmas time Melissa always felt happy and proud because a family custom made her the center of attention for at least a few important moments. This was because she was considered to be the lucky child in the family, just like her grandmother. On Christmas Eve, the custom was that Melissa had to leave the house through the back door and be the first person to enter the house holding a bible that was then read by the family together. This was supposed to bring the family good luck. Earlier, her grandmother used to do this for the family by walking through the door with a bottle of whiskey or wine. As Melissa indicated with a pleased smile, she enjoyed her special role very much. It made her feel important.

Melissa felt treasured, and lived up to the myth of being the bright child in the family like her granny. She added that it might sound strange to me, the interviewee, but even as a child she wanted her hair to become grey so that she could look like her granny. She wanted so much to be like her. Even after she had grown up, the roles in the family remained fixated. Melissa was beautiful and was allowed to study without interruption; no one expected her to do household chores. Consequently, she had a lot of free time. As an afterthought, she mentioned that she also resembled both an older brother who died when he was three months of age and her maternal grandmother—both very well loved in the family.

Transactions that take place in families involve familiar child-rearing and socializing functions. Many other aspects of the child's development are affected by their interactions within this subsystem. Family members learn to rely on other family members who have greater resources or strength. A young person's sense of self is determined by how family members respond to her or him at different stages of development. Members learn how to fight as well as how to negotiate.

As we look at the early life of Melissa, we see the formation of certain family myths which were reflected in her attitudes and behavior. One myth specified that mother was ill and everyone in the family had to cater to her. However, the overall family theme of the myth specified, "We are a happy family." It was apparent that the mother controlled the family through her heart condition and everyone performed their dance around the mother based on her needs. The coherence in this family was maintained through the roles created for each member—mother, the sick person; father, the quiet responsible person; Matilda, the home manager; Leonard, the fun child; Melissa, the pet and the bright child. Whatever matters had to be settled in the family, they would go to their mother and she would settle everything amicably for everyone. One of the myths in this family said that we do not get angry because we are happy people and "We are a happy family."

COMMUNICATION PATTERNS IN THE FAMILY

Every family has its own styles of communication, rules and regulations of behavior, and a philosophy of life that guide the socialization of its children.

Bateson (1979) described human relationships as a process of differentiation in the norms of individual behavior that results from cumulative interaction between the individual members. In this process, individuals develop mutual reactions to behavior. This important information about mutual causal processes evolved from Bateson's study of the Iatmul society. Bateson noted that when one person, called Pinah, behaved in a certain way towards Keeta, this triggered a particular kind of response from Keeta whose behavior in turn resulted in a certain response from Pinah, and so forth. Bateson called these schismogenic cycles and categorized these cycles into two groups called *symmetrical*, meaning that the escalating behavior of Pinah and Keeta would be similar, as in the case of rivalry and competition; or *complementary*, meaning that the self-generating patterns would be different, in cycles of dominance-submission.

Bateson (1979) further clarifies this concept by discussing the self-reinforcing patterns that result in various kinds of mental illness. In some, characterized by paranoia, the patient's suspiciousness triggers responses in others that serve to justify the person's fears and make him or her even more distrustful. In a marriage, when one partner is extremely assertive and the other is compliant, these characteristics may become progressively accentuated, with one partner becoming increasingly more compliant and the other becoming more and more assertive. I found this in the patterns of behavior the couples developed among themselves, especially as they got older.

Parents and children, also, develop self-perpetuating and self-escalating patterns that may be carried over into adult life. At times, when patterns are destructive, there are attempts to change and rearrange the patterns. However, this usually takes a lot of time and effort.

As Lederer and Jackson (1968) indicated, all behavior in families may be understood through communication—a constant exchange of information and messages between family members through speech and nonverbal interaction. Often, through tone of voice and gestures, we can understand the relationships that exist in the family. Information that is given and received is sometimes straightforward and factual, but at other times is complicated by the relationship between those involved. "I want a drink of water" may mean "I don't want to go to sleep" or "I would like you to cater to my needs" or "I want to change the subject." Messages as well as feelings are expressed in different ways: The rattling of pots in the kitchen and the slamming of a door could telegraph a person's mood. The raising of eyebrows, a frown, the bringing of flowers, the cooking of a person's favorite dish, a warm handshake, slamming a door, a kiss are examples of nonverbal messages that speak louder than words. As a child grows in a family, he or she learns to understand and utilize the unique communication patterns in that family.

Anger

Hostility is the social expression of anger. Hostility is the behavior; anger is the feeling.

Anger can be expressed in a variety of ways, ranging from mere change of facial expression or quiet verbal expression to a loud, self-consummating outpouring, depending upon the status and culture and experiences of a particular family. In our culture, "nice, respectable people" are expected to be "refined" in their expression of anger. Only animals roar. In our culture, we expect women to be more self-controlled and restrained in anger than men (Henry, 1965).

In this family there was no verbal expression of anger. Quarreling was viewed as degrading, and the culprit was made to feel ashamed. Moreover, any person who quarreled in this family would have to bear the burden of guilt and the family's silent wrath for threatening the mother's health and life. The real issue of what roles different members were playing and how they felt about them were overlooked. Henry (1965) indicates that when people are unassertive, they become tense and vigilant but rarely let their feelings out. This inner rage produces stored up resentment on the basis of their distorted perceptions and secret blame toward the secret enemy.

If anger is a taboo, a person may feel guilty or ashamed for feeling angry and try to avoid any overt expression of this emotion. In Melissa's case, she avoided any topic that was controversial in their family.

INITIAL CRISIS IN THE FAMILY

The family system was maintained on the belief that they were a happy family. Whenever I tried to get details about Melissa's relationship with her sister, it was obvious that there was discomfort and she would change the subject. There were apologetic comments that she did not understand her sister when she was young. She felt guilty because she never questioned the fact that her sister did all the housework and gave up dates in order to take care of her younger siblings. The family tradition said that Matilda was the oldest and therefore had to perform all the work in the family. As our interview sessions gained momentum, Melissa revealed that Matilda and her mother may not have really liked each other. When Matilda complained about having too much to do, her mother would tell her gently that if she cut her long hair she would not have to spend so much time washing it!

On further discussion, Melissa explained that her older sister was a great beauty. Moreover, she was in perfect health. Did the mother attempt to get back at her by making her the maid of the family? How is it that even as Melissa and her brother grew up they were never asked to pitch in? The father did not interfere in the mother-daughter relationship except when Matilda got angry with her mother for not doing any work in the house. If Matilda complained, the mother would develop breathing difficulties and this would leave her devastated. This, in turn, would upset the father who would punish Matilda by taking away her privilege of going out with friends. It appears that, besides being the homemaker, Matilda was also the scapegoat of the family.

The family faced a major crisis when Melissa was nine years

old. At that time, Matilda was 17 and terribly overworked. Melissa walked into the kitchen early one morning to talk to her sister. Instead she found a note that announced that her sister had run away from home. The family searched for her for a number of days. I asked Melissa if she was angry at the time. She replied negatively: "Why should I be angry, maybe she did the right thing." She was not angry nor did she have any ill feelings towards her sister. Whether this was her inability to express anger or her repression of any such feelings I could not tell. Melissa added with hesitation that her parents had said that nobody should talk about Matilda's flight in the family. After two weeks, she was found and brought home. She was dressed in gaudy clothes that she never got to wear at home and was pretty upset at being "caught."

After this first incident, there were many such incidents, but Melissa insisted that they were a happy family and her mother used to tell her that Matilda was a little "sick" in the head and that's why she behaved the way she did, and that it should not really affect the happiness of the family.

When Matilda was 19 she eloped with a man and later married him. This time she was gone for eight months. When she returned with her husband she was quickly forgiven. Again, there was denial of anger. They just missed her, she said. Matilda's husband was Jonathan, tall, goodlooking and arrogant.

How did the family manage without Matilda? The father started to participate in housework. Melissa did some housework and Clara, her mother, started to function as a housekeeper and cook, though she constantly needed help. Melissa was contemplative. She wondered how things would have been had their mother done housework while Matilda was still at home. Melissa did not do heavy housework as nobody wanted her to strain herself. During this period, her mother would become exhausted easily and everybody had to make sure she did not overstrain herself. More often than she cares to remember, Melissa wished that her older sister were home, but in retrospect, it looks as if they managed very well without her. After all, it did help them to get back together as a "happy family" when Matilda returned home.

Matilda ran away from home in anger and frustration, or both.

Due to the belief in this family about the mother's ill-health, there was no direct blaming. The myth of happiness was apparently aimed at maintaining the status quo, either by doing nothing or by blocking any action designed to produce changes in daily living and the relationships. There was a powerful and controlling "sick" mother and the peripheral father.

This family reflected the myth of harmony in spite of its problems: A beautiful picture is painted of the family's present and past togetherness, harmony and happiness.

TEEN YEARS

Melissa had dated two men. The first man was Scottish and the match was completely approved by her family and his family. After they had been engaged for a couple of months, Melissa, her fiancé and some friends went to the park. During the outing, her fiancé continuously tried to control her. This upset her so much that she decided she did not wish to marry him, much to her mother's grief. During this time, her older brother had married and moved out of the house.

Melissa's sister, Matilda, did not do well with her husband. After two children were born, they were divorced. Maybe Matilda should not have left home, that early, she whispered, wondering if this could be the reason her sister's marriage had failed. After Matilda's marriage ended, she did not visit her family at all and finally married another man from Canada whom they knew only through descriptions by mutual friends. Matilda never brought him home. Melissa added, "We were brought up as happy people but Matilda chose to keep her distance from us." It was only after many years and her mother's death that Matilda made an effort to be friendly with her sister and brother.

Though Melissa described her family as a happy one, there apparently existed a pseudomutuality that affected family roles. When there are unreal qualities of both positive and negative emotions, then the terms pseudomutuality and pseudohostility are used. Wynne et al. (1958) explain how these features operate in such families. There is an intense wish by family members for mutual relatedness which excludes the ability to tolerate difference or dissent. The illusion of "pseudomutuality" reinforces the idea that all are linked together. Children in such families are thus caught in the dilemma of never being able to differentiate or disengage because any attempt brings the expectation of disaster. Thus, there was fusion in the family and even when members physically left the home, they were still a part of it in their unexpressed anger, as seen in Matilda's case. I wonder if this anger was ever worked through or expressed since Matilda visited her parents' home only after her mother died.

Mother's Death

Melissa was 19 and dating a "fabulous" young man when her mother died. Clara was in her forties and had developed pneumonia, which was not treated properly. Before they knew it, she became seriously ill. On her deathbed, Clara made Melissa promise that she would take care of her father. Her brother, who lived in another state, came to visit his mother when he realized how ill she was. Though repeated messages were sent to the oldest daughter, Matilda, she did not come, to her parents' grief. Melissa apologized for her sister. Of course she must have had really important things to do. The fact that there was a lot of anger between Matilda and her mother was denied.

There is also the presence of white sham in this family—concealment and pretense that are merely socially necessary. White sham, as Henry (1965) points out, is used to preserve social relations. For example, a group of people may sit around a table and the air may be electric with mutual hostility and scorn; yet they put on pleasant faces and crack jokes and roar with laughter. There was much pain and unhappiness but the Simpson family members wore masks and kept insisting that they were a happy family.

Loyalty to the Family

Throughout the interviewing, Melissa repeated, "We never give up our family customs, we are a happy family and that's the way we will be." When Clara died, she left her wedding ring to her oldest daughter as this was the custom in their family. Melissa seemed resentful of this, as her sister was not around even when her mother was seriously ill, though she was sent repeated messages. I asked Melissa if she felt let down by her mother as Melissa was the person who had taken care of her when she was so ill. Melissa looked up and told me that she was happy that her older sister got it, and therefore did not feel any resentment towards her. There was denial or unawareness of such feelings though they obviously were there; she murmured, "Family traditions are family traditions." Though many years had passed since this incident, Melissa added uncomfortably, "The ring really did not bother me . . . I knew I was the family pet." She also romanticized her mother's death by talking about a pet bird of her mother's that died the day her mother died. She said that this bird was called Billy and was her mother's favorite pet. When she got ill, the bird also seemed to wither away, and when she died, it died too. The family decided never to have birds as pets because there was a feeling that the mother loved birds so much that they should always remain her exclusive possession.

Loyalty and indebtedness are important aspects of families and these were a part of Melissa's family pattern. The mother probably felt guilty at having overworked her daughter or had to live up to the myth of being the "beautiful lady" she was always considered to be. On her deathbed she carried out the family tradition and left her wedding ring to her oldest daughter.

How was this family bound together in loyalty and what did loyalty mean to the family members? In such situations, each person maintains a ledger of perceptions of the balances of past, present and future give and take. What has been "invested" in the family system through availability and what has been withdrawn in the form of support received or one's exploitative use of other people remain in the invisible accounts of obligations (Boszormenyi-Nagy and Spark, 1973). Loyalty, indebtedness and family tradition, all enveloped with family myths, played a part in the dying mother's giving her wedding ring to her parental but "negative" child.

ADULT YEARS

Melissa married an Irishman who was extremely caring and kind. Her father did not approve of the marriage because the man was a Catholic.

She loved Daniel very much and decided to go against her father's wishes. When she informed him of this he wished her happiness by commenting that he hoped that she would be a good Catholic, at least.

Her father and her brother did not attend the wedding though they lived close by at that time. How did this affect Melissa? She smiled, "You know we were a happy family and I knew it would not last." Six months after her marriage, her father and her brother came to visit her and everything was forgiven and forgotten. There was no mention of her sister, as if she did not exist. When I persistently questioned her about her sister, Melissa became uneasy and responded by once again revealing her family loyalty. She blamed Matilda's husband, saying that he was responsible for her not coming home, overlooking the fact that they did not have a great relationship even before this young man entered her sister's life. She mentioned that "he" changed her and so she did not seem to care for the family.

What about their earlier relationship? She said that Matilda's relationship was fine with everyone except her mother. There were dynamics of family loyalty and indebtedness that superseded individual psychodynamics. Inherent in families of close and meaningful relationships are fundamental elements of giving and receiving. Factors like martrydom, overgiving, overpaying or receiving with no possibility of giving back are all parts of the family system. Martyrdom or overgiving and permissiveness, scapegoating, and parentification are illustrations of nonbalancing or nonmutual reciprocity in family relationships. Such relationships stimulate feelings of despair since it becomes impossible to settle family accounts—neither through emotional interest and concern nor by concrete actions (Boszormenyi-Nagy and Spark, 1973). Thus, the need to blame not the sister but the brother-in-law who is an outsider.

How did her father and brother come to visit her after six months?

Melissa talked about the circumstances. She was expecting her first child, who was stillborn in the fifth month of pregnancy and she became seriously ill. Moreover, she started to develop heart pains that scared her husband, Daniel, and these pains continued for a long time. When her father was informed, he came with her brother and they were really sorry for forsaking her—even for so short a period of time.

Before their marriage, she reached an agreement with Daniel that he would allow her father to live with them, as she had promised this to her dying mother. An analysis of the ethical dimension of relationships begins with the recognition that mutual obligations and entitlements exist in all relationships. In all relationships, but particularly in families, the obligation varies depending upon the merit of the other person's claims.

Obligation and entitlement are inseparable. In any relationship, between two people, the balance of obligation and entitlement fluctuates constantly in response to their actions toward one another. Melissa saw herself as the favorite child of her family. She felt that she had fared better in her family of origin than any of the other children and therefore felt the obligation to take care of her father. It was a promise that she had made to her mother as well. Thus, her father became a member of her own household. She added that she had never disobeyed her father and the first time she did, it was only to marry the man of her dreams. Of course, they had a beautiful married life, everything was perfect, they did not ever have any fights or misunderstandings, her husband was a loving, caring person whom everyone loved, including her father. Her father and husband became really good friends. Melissa took good care of her father and he still continued to call her "granny" as her mother had done, because this reminded him of his home and wife. I was almost presented with a fairy-tale story. . . .

Melissa's Health

Melissa suffered from chest pains and feared that she might have a weak heart like her mother. This turned out to be true, yet Melissa gave birth to three children. Thus, I saw another generation where the mother controlled the family from her bed-side. Melissa's first pregnancy resulted in a stillbirth. Later she had another child, a beautiful girl named Mary Anne, with blonde hair and blue eyes, who developed a brain tumor and died at three years of age. While relating this, Melissa's eyes filled with tears. It was painful to have a child die so young. Finally, she had a healthy baby boy. Because of her poor health, she under-went sterilization. Thus, her son Donald became the only child in the family.

Melissa found that she did not have enough strength to go out by herself. As a result, she had both her husband and her father catering to all her needs. She spent a lot of her time knitting and reading books; she was the intellectual in the family. Her son grew up "without giving me any trouble." Thus, there was a carryover of the family myth from the family of origin into this family of procreation.

What about her husband's background? He was a quiet, shy person who came from a family of two children. He had a sister who was 12 years older than he was. In many ways he felt like an only child. He was basically a loner, doing things by himself. He enjoyed reading as well as going to baseball games. He was also a good dancer. She enjoyed doing these things with him when she could and was grateful that she had learned about baseball from her brother in her younger days.

She described herself as being the best child in the family in her youth and now in her old age as well. Her brother divorced his wife after ten years of marriage. Melissa commented that his wife was not a good person, but did not wish to go into details. Within a short time he married another beautiful woman who was "almost perfect." I noticed as I talked to Melissa that terms like "perfect" and "always happy" popped up continuously.

Melissa felt that she was the "best" because she was happily married and had not been divorced. Why did two out of three marriages in this family, which believed in calling itself the happy family, fail? One can trace the reasons to the fact that each part-ner enters a marriage situation with a set of rules and needs that they wish to fulfill in the marital situation. Neither partner ever merely responds to the other person. Both try to fulfill their own needs as well as the partner's ambivalent and defensive needs. Both respond to and affect each other in their exquisite, unconscious sensitivity. To blame one or the other would be a distortion of reality that fails to appreciate the marital system. Each member of the couple must develop a "no fault" attitude as they learn that their interactions may work both positively and negatively on their own behalf and on the marriage (Karpel and Strauss, 1983).

In this interaction, each partner is attempting to achieve his or her own fulfillment of the individual contract, including ambivalences and self-imposed deterrents to fulfillment. Each person wants more from the partner than from anyone else in the world and each is willing to give something in exchange for what he or she wants. So they play games with each other based on testing, faith, teasing, love, suspicion, coercion, threats, manipulation and a thousand other ways of attempting to get what they think they want or to see that the wife or husband does not get what she or he wants. Partners try to elicit reactions from each other that will fulfill their fondest dreams as well as their worst fears (Sager, 1976).

Some relationships satisfy the needs of both spouses and bring about a feeling of happiness and pleasure along with the sense of pain that is occasionally experienced. Others do not fulfill the purposes of the individual or system, or fulfill them at the expense of one or both of the partners. There is pain or emptiness when one is sharing a life with an enemy and not a friend (Boszormenyi-Nagy and Spark, 1973). Divorces result and, at times, beside the pain that accompanies the breakup of a relationship, there is relief that the bad relationship has been dealt with.

As for Melissa's siblings, it appeared as if Melissa blamed their spouses, not them, due to family loyalties and obligations. People do make inappropriate claims in relationships and the willingness of one party to capitulate to unilateral, excessive claims may be as harmful in the long-term interests of the relationship as an unwillingness to consider any claims. In Melissa's family of origin, she had her way more often than her husband had in his family. As a result, more members of her family of origin than her husband's visited them and the boundaries between herself, her father and her siblings were fairly diffused. In her husband's case, he had moved away from his hometown and did not visit his family often.

Middle Years and Relationship with Family

Melissa spent a lot of her time in bed, as her mother had, and was well taken care of by her father and her husband. If the men had any negative feelings toward each other, it was never revealed to Melissa. She felt they got along very well. Often, the notion of a romantic marriage rests on the myth of complete harmony or togetherness. In actuality, the development of some autonomy is inevitable and desirable. However, some forms of independent expression or activity are more acceptable to a particular husband and wife than others. Melissa believed in the myth of happiness and could not allow herself to perceive any conflicts.

Melissa described her son, Donald, as handsome and easy to be with. She also felt that her dead daughter, Mary Anne, whom she loved very much, was her brother's guardian angel and took care of him so that he would never get into any trouble. She added dreamily that she had planted evergreens for her daughter in every house she lived in. She felt that her daughter's spirit lived with them and felt her presence very strongly, particularly when she was ill. To my question, "Did you feel this when you were sad?" she responded with a smile, "I was never really sad." I was up against the myth of harmony and happiness once again.

Melissa described her son as resembling her grandmother and herself but she avoided calling him "granny" because he was a boy. However, the temptation never left her. Her son, unlike her husband who worked in a factory, went on to college with her intellectual help in preparing applications, as she was the bright one in the family. He managed to get into a good university and obtained an engineering degree. She described him as a pleasant and decent human being who did not give any trouble, as well as being a good student and hard worker.

While she was in her forties, her father, who was in his seventies, fell down and never recovered from his injury and its complications. He died in his sleep three months later. Her brother and sister came for the funeral. It was sad but they felt that he had led a good life. Her sister was still beautiful to look at, but she spent a lot of time during the funeral drinking in the kitchen. She explained that she was tired from her journey from Canada, as well as sad at her father's death. However, Melissa added, they were a happy family and it was right that her father died at her house as she was the happiest among her siblings and of course the parents' favorite.

As often seen among the families of the elderly who were interviewed, the favorite child became the parentified child as the siblings left home, and then took over the major responsibility of caring for or visiting the parent. In this case, the father lived with the favorite child till he died.

Life Without Daniel

After her father's death, it appeared as if there was a vacuum in Melissa's family. Her husband stayed away from home more often and her son took care of her when she felt ill. However, she insisted they were happy people and did not have any problems. When her husband was about 63 years of age, he had a heart attack and died. It was sudden and almost before they knew what had happened he was gone. It was ironic that Melissa had suffered from heart problems from the time she was young, but her husband had just one attack and died. As hard as I tried, I could not get Melissa to talk about this period in any detail. She kept saying that she was happy she had her son.

During this period her son decided to get married. He chose a girl, Mary, who was a neighbor's daughter, and Melissa was pleased. After the marriage, they left for Texas, leaving Melissa lonely and sad. She who had always complained of heart problems found herself working for the telephone company. She needed the money and said she felt well. What about her heart problem? Well, it was not too serious, she responded.

During this period her older brother, who lived about 40 miles away, died in a car accident. It was sad, but "That's life," she added. Her sister, Matilda, started to visit her more often. She was an alcoholic, and retained the label of the bad child in the family. She would visit to borrow money from Melissa, but would never repay it. One day Melissa asked her for it. Matilda retorted that Melissa was paying her for all the work that Matilda had done for her as a child. This upset Melissa, but her sister never returned to see her. She quickly added that they still corresponded with each other and she still loved her sister very much. Nowadays it was Matilda's daughter who kept in touch with Melissa and gave her all the news about her sister and brother-in-law. She described her sister as having mellowed somewhat; she was nicer and kinder to family and friends at present than she had ever been.

Melissa's Second Marriage

Melissa was lonely and one day she met some friends of her husband's with whom they used to play cards. She was happy to have some company and enjoyed being with this couple. She added that she had decided never to remarry. She had been married once and that was enough. Her son kept in touch with her sporadically. She was pleased that he and his wife were happy. They had two sons but no daughters. Melissa's voice trailed away when she added that if they had had a daughter, maybe they would have called her "granny." She began to spend more and more time with this couple, Edward and Maria, who were Irish Catholic like her husband. One day, Edward told her that his wife had had a third heart attack and was in the hospital. At first Melissa did not take it seriously, since she herself had had so many "heart attacks," as had her mother. However, four days later, Maria died. Melissa was both sad and surprised.

Edward came to see her more often and one year later, some seven years after she had been widowed, Melissa remarried. She described herself as happy and added that they were a great pair and they felt like "lovebirds." A few years later her husband had a stroke and she began suffering from swollen legs, so they moved into the nursing home together. While we talked, her husband sat in the corner of the room, listening to us and participating off and on. He commented that she was a good wife. She topped him loudly by saying that they had the most beautiful companionship that anyone could ever imagine. Incidentally, Edward could not talk well, as he had undergone an operation on his throat. I thought it easy to be "lovebirds" when only one spoke. Melissa mentioned that they were a happy couple and a happy family, as her son who had approved of this marriage would send his wife to visit them at least once a year and if he passed by New York, he would drop in himself.

Though everything about this family revealed that there was a lot of strife and anger, it was generally pushed under the rug because family members really believed that they were a happy family. Often an explanation that sounded superficial to an outsider was real to this family, because it served the protective and defensive functions of the family by retaining the myth of harmony and togetherness.

Another important factor that struck me was that Melissa spoke very little about any important people in her life outside the nuclear family, except for her grandmother. There was no interest in talking about other relatives and friends. It was as if her life's energy had been and still was being consumed in her immediate family and its life history, with the constant need in Melissa to prove that she had always done the right thing for her parents and the rest of the family. If her sister was not in touch with her, she was in touch with her sister's daughter. The money that her sister borrowed was never returned, but what did it matter, they were still loyal to each other; perhaps there was guilt in Melissa, for having been the favored daughter and the pet of the family?

POSTSCRIPT

I went back to see Melissa about 15 months later. Melissa had suffered a heart attack and was in bed. Her husband was sitting close by. The nurse told me that it was a mild attack and she would recover. I went back to see Melissa the following week and we talked for a while. She was pleasant as usual, and she mentioned that her sister had died of liver trouble during the past year. She added that her sister drank a lot. She also noted that she was the last one left in her family of origin. We discussed some of the earlier life history material and though Melissa was in her early seventies, her memory was still sharp. After a few hours, she told me pleasantly, ''I hope you will be happy and have a happy family like I did.'' I smiled and waved goodbye. The myth was still alive.

CHAPTER 6

In the Life of John Howard

He looked much younger than I expected, a tall thin man with a handsome, smiling face. I put out my hand to shake his as he struggled in his chair attempting to sit upright. John smiled, "I'm glad to see you, I hope I am not the only person you wished to talk to, again?" "No, why do you say that?" "Well, I just wondered . . ."

EARLY HISTORY

John was the younger of two children. His mother, Lillian, was Irish and his father, Patrick, was Irish and English. His mother came from a large family with five girls and two boys; his father had one brother. Patrick married Lillian, a small town girl, whom he had known for a long time. In this family, Patrick was considered to be a very handsome man who could get away with anything because of his good looks. He spent a lot of time away from home, held jobs off and on, and in any problematic situation, he had his brother and father to fall back on. Patrick was his father's favorite son. He was an extremely friendly person whom everyone liked. He was also known as a lady's man whom marriage did not hold back in any way. Men were guys to whom women catered—this was the myth in this family.

FAMILY TREE OF JOHN HOWARD

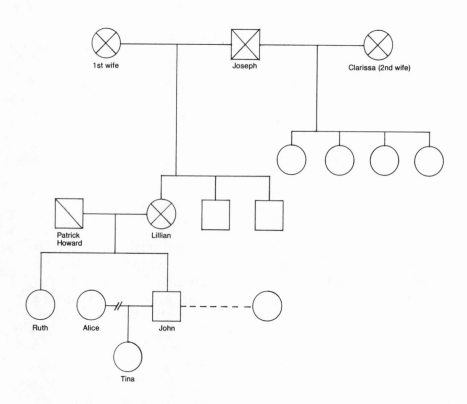

Every family is a rule-governed system and members, irrespective of their family life-styles, behave themselves in an organized, repetitive manner. This patterning of behaviors can be abstracted as a governing principle of family life (Watzlawick and Weakland, 1977). Family rules are learned through practice and mastered as part of family culture.

Lillian was a retiring person who did not interfere in her husband's life. She came from a family where her mother died when she was a young child and her father remarried within a short period of time. Lillian had four stepsisters and two natural brothers. According to what John heard from his mother, she was not treated well as a young person. Her father was dependent on her. She was the oldest and had looked after her two younger brothers before her father remarried. She continued to feel responsible for her younger brothers even after her father remarried. This made her stepmother, Clarissa, angry. Lillian was often caught in the middle of quarrels between her stepmother and her father and was frequently blamed for these quarrels. It appeared that, developmentally, Lillian was caught in a triangulation situation between her mother and her father.

As Bowen (1976) describes it, the theory states that a triangle is a three-person emotional configuration which is the molecule or the building block of any emotional system, whether it is the family or any other group. The triangle can be described as the smallest stable relationship system. A two-person system is stable as long as it is calm, but when anxiety increases, it immediately causes the most vulnerable member to reach another person, resulting in a triangle. When tension becomes too great for the threesome, it involves others to become a series of interlocking triangles.

In Lillian's family of origin, it was Lillian who obviously was the third person in the triangle. This fusion of the child with the emotional relationship system of a family triangle inhibits the child's normal process of differentiation of intellect and emotion (Bowen, 1976). Thus, when her father and stepmother had misunderstandings, Lillian was upset for she felt herself constantly caught between them.

Patterns repeat themselves in triangles and people come to have fixed roles in relation to each other. An example of this is the father-mother-child triangle. The common pattern in Lillian's family of origin was that the father was weak and passive, taking the outsider's position and leaving the conflict between the mother and daughter. The stepmother in this case was domineering and aggressive and constantly gave Lillian a hard time. This left Lillian emotionally scarred long after she had left the home of origin. She could never stand up to her husband, Patrick. She felt vulnerable and avoided visiting her parents completely. Perhaps she felt like an outsider, too, as the number of stepsiblings increased. The relationship between her and her stepsiblings was strained most of her life though she kept in touch with her natural brothers. Lillian played housemaid and homemaker as long as she could remember in her parents' house. Thus, her relationship with her parents was polarized, though apparently there was an alignment between her and her father while she was a member of that family.

John reminisced that he did not see much of his grandparents from his mother's side, but heard a number of stories about his mother's childhood from her that always made him sad. She was happy to marry Patrick, a good-looking man who worked on the railroad and lived away from her immediate neighborhood. After she left her family of origin, there was an impervious barrier to her entering it physically again as she was soon made to feel an outsider. She was grateful to have a home and made few demands on Patrick, especially since he took good care of her in terms of economic necessities. Thus, we see two individuals being united but coming from two different types of family dances. It appeared as if in Patrick's home "dances with joy" were more common, unlike Lillian's home where there were more "dances of pain."

When people dance, they express themselves. Lillian's family of origin dance could be compared to the Maori dances (Haskell, 1969), which are war dances and particularly fierce, with tempo marked by the beating of the palms or thighs, the pulling of faces already grotesque with tatoo marks, and the defiant thrusting out of the tongue. It appeared as if Patrick came from a family that performed ballet, in the sense that their dancing was light, graceful, and supple, with a flexible movement of the limbs. In addition, the male dancers must be strong to lift a ballerina effortlessly to shoulder height, to leap with vitality when necessary, and to land with grace. This was true of Patrick's family of origin: The men enjoyed their "independence" but took good care of their family members.

Life at Home

John's mother took care of him, but it was his father who captured John's heart and head. After all he was a man like his father.

John witnessed his father's behavior and habits. As a child, he had often gone out with his father and listened to him tell jokes and brag to his friends about "things that he had done," washing down their conversations with hard drinks. John wonders now why he was not treated as a child and kept away. The boundaries between father and son appeared diffused. As Minuchin (1974) puts it, boundaries are created to protect the differentiation of the system; here the boundaries between father and son had not yet been established and differentiation was a long way off. Every family subsystem has some specific functions to perform and makes specific demands upon its members. The development of interpersonal skills achieved in these subsystems can be predicted based on the subsystem's freedom from interference from other subsystems. Minuchin postulates that there are three types of boundaries: enmeshed/diffused, disengaged/rigid, and clear.

As the term "diffused" implies, in this father-son relationship the boundaries between them were ambiguous and not well maintained. Thus, the boundaries separating parents and children were frequently invaded in improper ways, as will be seen, and the roles of spouse and parent were never clearly differentiated. The result was that neither the spouse subsystem nor the parent subsystem operated with ease.

Finally, the children were not differentiated on the basis of age or maturational level, so that the sibling subsystem did not contribute properly to the socialization process (Hoffman, 1981). John mentioned that he and his father did not go to church because neither of them liked closed places. He added, jokingly, that they could be suffering from claustrophobia; anything that was closed would turn them off. They loved open places and fresh air. With a twinkle in his eyes, John went on to mention that he and his father were the two people in the family who did not go to confession, much to the grief of his mother who was a religious person.

This was the only area that appeared to create overt conflict for the couple. Lillian was a strict Catholic and resented that Patrick did not go to church. Often, John would be used as the mediator and buffer when the father would try to convince his wife that he and his son were uncomfortable in closed places.

"Is this true, now?" I asked John. "No, no, not at all," John commented.

Thus, John was the link between the parents in this part of their lives and had great difficulty in rejecting this role. Moreover, from a young age, John saw himself as an ally of his father. As Willi (1982) specifies, when partner A joins C as his ally, receiving support from him or her in his battle against partner B, B feels betrayed and tries to find an ally for herself, thus expanding further the circle of conflict. This unilateral ally usually adds to the dyadic friction, aiding one parent at the expense of the other. Unilateral turning towards a third person in a situation is one of the most common and perhaps most dangerous coping maneuvers, both on psychological and social grounds. Moreover, it runs counter to two principles that Willi believes are important in a healthy marriage. The demarcation principle is undermined by the initiation of an exclusive relationship aimed against the marital partner. Similarly, the balance of equal worth is upset by one of the partners arbitrarily elevating his or her position by involving a third person. This makes the other person feel defeated and betrayed, and forced to take countermeasures in order to restore the balance (Willi, 1982).

John had an exclusive relationship with his father within the family. He remembered spending hours with his father's friends while they sang songs and played the guitar. How did his mother view this? If she even so much as commented on it, it would make his father angry and he would jump to the defense of his son. Often he would ridicule his wife to his son, saying that he was a man and should not be cowed by a woman, even if it was his mother. This was the type of relationship style that John grew up with.

The concept of role, although useful, does not really address the most basic feelings and motives that provide meaning and direction to family relationships. It is useful to look upon the family as the matrix of identity—the primary source of self. The "self" might be viewed as the result of countless interactions between an individual and significant others. The latter are people who are so vitally related to a person that they hold survival value for him or her—socially, emotionally and ultimately—through psychosomatic mechanisms, physically as well as psychically (Watzlawick and Weakland, 1977).

The members of one's family are one's significant others par excellence. Particularly in the formative years, the development of a person's self-concept is highly connected to the manner in which family members relate to him or her. The quality of personal affirmation or rejection in the formative years has an impact upon an adult's behavior patterns in relation to friends, occupation, mate selection, and the formation of a person's own marriage and family system.

The development of a person's identity, rests on two basic crucial human experiences: belonging and separateness. Belonging is the basic human need for affirmation and acceptance by a group of important people. Inseparable from this experience of belongingness is the person's need to be recognized as unique and relatively autonomous. A family's style of responding to individual differences in thoughts, feelings, intentions, and actions has important consequences in a person's development. When this existential dimension is added to the concept of role reciprocity or interrelatedness, one is better able to appreciate the tremendous importance of family interaction patterns.

John's sister, Ruth, was a timid, shy girl, not half as good-looking as her brother. Her worst feature was her nose "that hung like a heavy piece of flesh on her face." Then John laughed as he added, "It was not that bad, but that's how they made Ruth feel." She was not as good-looking as her brother but was constantly compared to him and put down. She was awkward and shy and continued to be that way even in her old age. Her nickname at home was "Nosy" and John would tease her when he wanted to get her irritated. John was considered to be the "cute one" in the family and everyone loved him very much. As long as John could remember, he was the center of attention as a child and he got more of everything in comparison to his sister. He could also get away with a lot of mischief because he was a boy.

The relationship between John and his sister was not positive.

If John did not go to church, his mother would sulk because she could not control him; she would have her daughter as an ally. Thus, coalitions were developed in the family and when there was periodic escalation of hostilities between husband and wife, the children were part of it. Thus, there appeared to be a truce between the parents, with the children as allies.

In discussing cross-generation coalitions, Haley (1976) notes that they never occur alone but always in pairs. Particularly in disturbed families, a coalition of a parent with a child will often be matched by a coalition of another parent with a grandparent, or a child with a grandparent against the parent! The parent is the "bad guy" because he/she was a difficult child and a strict parent. However, in this case, the children are of the same generation. Haley further hypothesizes that the cause of many behaviors which in the past had been thought to be motivated by an individual's unhappiness or anger can be better understood in the larger context of family dynamics. A husband may join a son against his wife not only because he is unhappy with the wife but because a good relationship with his wife would have a disruptive effect on his relationship with his parents or, as in this case, with his son.

Ruth was older than John by four years, but had a low status in the family because of her "nose." John was the cute one and could entertain the family or his father's friends for hours with his jokes and laughter. On the other hand, his timid sister was ignored. Without hesitation, he added that he was the favorite of both his parents, though at times his mother and sister would do things together, particularly when it was connected to church. On reflection, John felt that his sister was included in the church activities only because he did not want to be part of them. He received more gifts from his parents and from relatives. Often, his sister would pick a fight with him, accusing him of turning her parents away from her. "Of course," he added "this would upset me," and he would complain to his parents and Ruth would be punished because she was the older child and should know how to behave herself.

Sibling Feelings

Minuchin and Fishman (1982) describe the sibling system as the first social laboratory in which children can experiment with peer relationships. Within this context they support each other, attack, enjoy, scapegoat, and generally learn from each other. They develop their own transactional process for negotiating, cooperating, and competing. It is in the family that children learn to prepare themselves for varieties of boundary negotiations. Minuchin emphasizes that what happens in the process is important, not why it happens. Children organize themselves into a variety of subsystems according to developmental stages. Depending upon age, sibling rivalry feelings are present in a number of areas such as autonomy, competition, and competence. But in this family, the siblings had been set apart from each other from the time they were young because of the different perceptions that the adult family members had of their sex roles.

John enjoyed the role he played in the family. He just had to be funny and cute and he had everyone dancing to his tunes. He was encouraged to behave in this manner from early childhood by the positive feedback he received from his family. His father frequently said, ''He's my son and he will grow up to be just like me.'' John was silent for a few moments. He mused and then added, ''I can still hear my father's voice saying these things as if it was only a few days ago.'' John was in his early seventies. How powerful families are, I thought.

Thus, the family structuring took place. John was the ''pet'' and ''good'' child and his sister the ugly child and scapegoat of the family as well. John could get away with all types of behavior because he was a boy and this family believed that they should be lenient with sons and strict with daughters. In this family, the family myth describes roles and attributes of family members in their transactions with each other which, although false and mirage-like, are accepted by everyone in the family as sacred (Ferreira, 1963) and are not challenged. This myth indicates that men are strong and women are weak. At a young age, John learned to enjoy his power over his sister as well as over his mother. The women gave in to him, easily because he was just like his father, a charmer.

As outlined by Carter and McGoldrick (1982) the normal family includes a vertical and a horizontal axis. The vertical flow in the system includes patterns of relating and functioning that are transmitted down the generations in a family primarily through the mechanisms of emotional triangling. It includes all family attitudes, taboos, expectations, labels, and loaded issues with which people grow up. One can say that these aspects of people's lives are like the hands dealt in a game of cards. What people choose to do with them is the issue.

The horizontal flow in the system includes the anxiety produced by the stresses on the family as it moves forward through time, coping with the changes and transitions of the family life cycle. It includes both the predictable developmental stresses as well as those unpredictable events that disrupt the family life cycle, like untimely death, birth of a disabled child, chronic illness, and so forth. If there is enough stress on a horizontal axis, any family will appear to be extremely dysfunctional. If there is stress combined from a horizontal and vertical axis, it will create a major disruption in the system. As we proceed, we will focus on the vertical axis that affects John Howard's life-style, referring to the horizontal axis when necessary.

Some Meaningful Childhood Memories

Some of the most pleasant memories John has of his childhood relate to the visits the family used to make to his father's brother who had a 220-acre farm where he could do very much what he wanted. He learned to connect this place in his mind to festive times such as Thanksgiving. His father's brother stood out in his mind as kind, caring, and indulgent. This uncle, Harry, did not have any children and therefore devoted a lot of time to John and his sister. Patrick's relatives worked on the railroad and they were kind and good people, but the only relative John remembers distinctly was his uncle, Harry.

On his mother's side, he did not seem to have any strong ties.

He brushed aside this relationship, saying that family relationships were strained and died out after his grandfather remarried. However, he was in touch with one of his mother's brothers who lived in Buffalo. John used to visit him fairly frequently and had a good relationship with him.

John did not like going to school because he wanted to study French and the school forced him to study Latin. This upset him so severely that he decided to leave school. His father set only one rule for leaving school—that John take a job immediately, which John did. Of course, he had regrets that he did not get past the seventh grade. However, he enjoyed working and made special mention of the coffee breaks when he and his friends would go out to eat, drink, and socialize. He remembers this period as a funfilled and happy period in his life. The most important figure in his life continued to be his father; they were friends besides being father and son. His memory of his mother was that of a caretaker who was always in the kitchen or praying.

DEVELOPMENTAL FRAMEWORK

Developmentally, there was denial of strength in women, by both the men and the women. John's mother, Lillian, appeared to be the captive audience in this family and she did not have the strength to fight for her rights or position. The couple had developed an organized way of behaving with each other. People who organize themselves together form a status, or power ladder in which each person has a place in the hierarchy, with someone above and someone below. Haley (1964) indicates that groups have more than one hierarchy because of different functions. The existence of hierarchy is inevitable because it is in the nature of organization to be hierarchical. Hierarchy is shaped by the people involved. Insofar as the behavior is repetitive and redundant, it is a governed system that is error-activated in that deviance activates a governing process. If a person deviates from the repeating behavior and so defines a different hierarchy, the others react against that deviation and shape the behavior back into a habitual pattern.

The hierarchy in this family specified that men had more power and control and women had to obey them. In her husband's house, Lillian denied the strengths that she had used in her family of origin as this had eventually led to her total rejection by her family of origin except by her natural brothers. Thus, she appeared to be a timid woman who let her husband control her. John's father came from a family where women were subordinated and this was carried over in John's family as well. It appeared that in this family men had the need to possess and be in control. John's sister, Ruth, as she grew older, slowly withdrew herself from her family and became an outsider.

Each family member developed a basic pattern of functioning within the family group that extended to participation in the broader society. When we look at the fabric of John's life, we become aware of the multiplicity of factors that influenced him. These included his own modes of feelings, thought, and action, as well as the cultural, economic, and political contexts in which his family functioned.

John's life structuring was a special kind of dance where women were considered to be weak and dependent. This helped to maintain the coherence of the family. There was denial of strength among the women and this appeared to be a loyalty-related alignment. Thus, this family myth functioned as a family compromise and defense. The family's developmental structure was an open sociocultural system that integrated the demands of society with those of the internal family system in shaping the individual. The process of birth, childhood, and adolescence, leaving one's family of origin, coupling, and beginning the process all over again with a new generation of children, after which one moves on toward later adult life, decline, and death, is a circular self-generating one.

How did this evolution take place in John's family of origin? The father, Patrick, was a strong, extremely good-looking man who engaged frequently in extramarital relationships. If his wife was aware of this, she handled it by becoming extremely religious and viewing it as the will of God. Thus there was an insecure, anxious wife who carried the responsibility of the family while her charming, braggart husband held the center of the stage.

Patrick had a life that had no limits in terms of responsibility to his marriage; between him and his wife a closeness-distance relationship existed. However, there were endless "quibbles" between them. Communication patterns and problems were frequently related to inability to tolerate closeness. The mother viewed the father as controlling and would withdraw when he questioned her about anything, complaining that his behavior was intrusive. How did John understand this? There were constant quarrels in the family and often he would notice his father pursuing his mother from the kitchen and to the bedroom while she avoided responding to him. Patrick would roar with drunken anger until his wife responded to him. John saw his mother as passive and his father as active.

Transactions within the parental holon involved the familiar childrearing and socializing functions. Many aspects of children's development are affected by their interactions within this subsystem. Children learn what to expect from people who have greater resources and strength, whether to think of authority as rational or arbitrary, how to communicate their wants and needs to other family members, and how these wants and needs will be met. Their sense of adequacy is shaped by how elders respond to them and whether this response is age-appropriate. Children learn which behaviors would be rewarded and which would be discouraged or punished. Finally, within the parental subsystem, the child experiences his or her family's style of dealing with conflict and negotiation (Minuchin and Fishman, 1982). The familiar stereotype of the virile but insensitive working-class husband and his long suffering wife who grimly performs her sexual duties appeared to fit this family (Komarovsky, 1964).

There was also the presence of the dominance-submission continuum where the wife was viewed as subordinate and the husband as dominant. In this family, gender role seemed to play an important part. Sex differences in any culture are the result of the interaction between biological inheritance and social learning. Males in this family were viewed as aggressive and adventurous, whereas women were viewed as being more accepting and nurturing. In this home, as in most homes, the sons used the father as a model. "My father never stayed home. He had a lot of fun outside of our home."

The models boys in our culture are encouraged to admire are aggressive types—policeman, pirates, bandits, and so forth. It is questionable if the values and standards derived from fantasy models rather than from real people are of positive assistance in enhancing social adjustment in later childhood and adulthood (Bentovim, Barnes and Cooklin, 1982). Daughters have fewer difficulties when it comes to role models. They usually follow the mother's leads and develop patterns of behavior that stress sociability, conformity, cooperation, submission, compliance, interest in domestic activities, and the use of verbal skills. These role patterns are reinforced when they enter school.

John was drinking by the time he was 12 years of age. He started to go out with girls when he was 14. His father encouraged him wholeheartedly, saying that a man had to experience the world. He loved his father, who continued to have exploits with women throughout John's youth. He identified with and admired him. He described his mother as a "weak woman" with whom his father could get away with anything. "Of course, what could women do; they were helpless and dependent." There was a close relationship between John and his father which even included discussion of their respective "conquests" of women.

There were no restrictions on John's behavior. He could go where he wanted and be back when he pleased. He enjoyed his freedom. John remembered his youth as a happy time except for his relationship with his sister.

TEEN YEARS AND MARRIAGE

John dated a number of girls but the person he remembers most was a college graduate from a very well-to-do family. It almost appeared that he would marry her, but when her parents objected, she became fearful and dropped him. Alice, the woman he married, was the result of a "family arrangement." He met her at his uncle's house and was invited there every weekend. She was quiet and timid, with dark hair and dark eyes, and he felt she would make a good wife. She came from a close-knit family of three sisters and two brothers.

After dating Alice for a couple of years, he married her when he was 20 years of age. He was happy for about three years and then matters began to change. He found her parents and her siblings were interfering in his life. They questioned him on his behavior and on things which he felt were none of their business. Of course, he was dating other girls on the side, but what was wrong with that? After all, his father had done the same and his mother hadn't seemed to mind; the role of a woman was to please and satisfy her man.

John felt that his wife failed him, miserably. She was so different from the girl he married. He expected her to be caring, but she would pick a quarrel on the smallest pretext. She was quarrelsome and angry most of the time. She would constantly question his behavior. He was aware that she did this because they did not have children. To get rid of all the outside pressures, he decided that they should have a child. This was based on the belief that a child would hold a marriage together. Women like children and know how to take care of them. Alice would spend her time caring for children and this would keep her occupied. Furthermore, he faced pressure from her family to have a child. The birth of a child appeared to smooth things out for a time. John loved his daughter, Tina. She was not as good-looking as he was since she resembled her mother, but she was bright and personable like him. Slowly he fell out of love with his wife.

Space

One of the techniques that both John and Alice used was buffering. This is a defensive maneuver in which one moves away from a threatening person or situation. Dodging, escaping, avoiding, and distancing all suggest unilateral buffering tactics. This was a common phenomenon in John's house. Either he avoided his wife or she avoided him.

Time

Time is a variable of behavior that is often taken for granted by both theoreticians and clinicians. Because time is so ever-present and yet so differently experienced, it is seldom dealt with in detail as a locus of interest in itself. Time orientation is the selection, directing, and maintaining of attitudes and behaviors toward the past, present, future, as well as toward non-temporal realms of experience by emphasizing one or more of these realms or the particular relationships among them. Where a family lives in *time* is as important as where it lives in *space* (Kantor and Lehr, 1975). John and his wife were temporally and spatially divergent from each other.

Clocking

Clocking is the regulation of the sequence, frequency, duration, and pace of immediately experienced events from moment to moment, hour to hour, and day to day. Clocking is concerned with the daily cycles of time, or with those cycles occurring within a day. Clocking phenomena are among the most immediate, poignant, and observable influences on behavior. If people are out of phase with one another, they may not even be able to be home together at the same time, much less make love to each other or fight with one another. Every experience is affected in one way or another by the way in which the family regulates its members' clocking. Whether a person feels his or her day is well spent, whether a man and woman can make love satisfactorily, and whether a family can spend time together in household chores or at play are all, in part, a question of clocking (Kantor and Lehr, 1975). In this family, the husband and wife were clearly out of phase. When the husband wanted to have a hearty breakfast, the wife avoided this activity by buffering as she disliked breakfasts and would have preferred to have an early lunch.

John continued to enjoy going out with other women and it did not matter to him that he was being unfaithful to his wife. He viewed marriage as a way of begetting children and his wife as a woman who kept house for him. He felt that he was providing well for them. He figured that his wife should not worry about his love life, but she did. They started to have violent quarrels. He was surprised whenever his wife responded to him in anger. He could not believe or accept it. He was mystified. The state of mystification is a feeling of being muddled or confused (Boszormenyi-Nagy and Framo, 1965). This seemed true in John's marital relationship. It was as if they as a couple could not dance together.

A marital identity evolves out of a commitment to an exclusive, specific, permanent relationship. In Erikson's (1959) view, young people are not ready to make this judgment before they have made certain basic decisions about themselves. The choice of a single-partner is the end of a search for temporary satisfaction and self-confirmation. This is replaced by a desire to form a single, lasting relationship, to take up challenges together with the other person, and to share a common path through life as a couple. The couple relationship is characterized by exclusivity, both with respect to the families of each partner and to other possible partners (Willi, 1982).

It appeared that John did not have a real commitment to this relationship and had patterned it in his mind after his father's life-style, which did not, however, suit his wife. It was taboo in his family of origin for women to have a point of view in worldly matters and his wife was violating this rule. His mother had taken a restricted role and played it very well. Thus, his family of origin, as a living system, exchanged information and energy with his world in which women and men had fixed roles.

Fluctuation in families, either internal or external, is normally followed by a response that returns the system to its steady state (Minuchin and Fishman, 1982). But this was not true in John's case. The spouses did not develop boundary relationships that would allow for satisfying patterns of transactions between themselves so that they could cope adequately with everyday life, that is, housework and sex. They had not renegotiated their boundaries and separated themselves from their families of origin. John had not made a firm commitment to the vows of marriage and perhaps this was never discussed. He learned to get secretive and did things on the sly. After all, he was an attractive man and women always found him irresistible. However, with his wife's large number of brothers and sisters, it was practically impossible for him to do anything without one of them spying on him. He was "sick" of all of them. His wife would moralize about the fact that they should lead honest, good lives and be good Christians; obviously, from Alice's point of view her husband did not have these qualities. Differences of opinion and lack of compatibility were leading this couple into a war dance. John and his wife quarrelled with each other, violently and constantly.

John's wife, Alice, appeared to be a dependent woman, but based her dependence on her mother and her siblings though she lived with John. Her emotional dependence upon her mother increased the potency of other disturbing conditions. A dependent wife tends to create situations in which the husband's will is pitted against the will of the mother-in-law. When a wife is under the influence of her mother, a disagreement between her mother and her husband leads to in-law conflict in areas in which a couple might have to make joint decisions. With a dependent wife, it becomes important that the husband and his mother-in-law become more congenial. However, in this marital situation this did not seem possible because all the in-laws were united against John. He did not have much family to fall back on. His sister was married and lived at that time on the outskirts of Buffalo where they originally came from.

While John was facing the difficulties in his marriage, he got the news that his father had been killed in a car accident. He was shocked and frightened. Though his father now played a less important role in his life in the physical sense, he was an irreplaceable person and a relational source. Bereavement and mourning are directly affected by the family's culture and this was true in John's case. He realized at this point in his life the lonely life he had led. Though he was in pain and anguish, he could not share this with his wife, who was aloof and distant. Things took a worse turn when his mother, who was ailing with cancer, died the following year. He grieved for his parents' death but also for his own pain and sorrow. There was no support from his wife. Of course he did not expect it. After all, she was a woman and how could she help him? He was alone.

Meanwhile, his marital life was becoming intolerable. He resented the fact that his in-laws interfered so much in his marriage. They lived next door and made it their business to pry into his family affairs. He was uncomfortable when the in-laws took sides with his wife; she listened to them rather than to her husband. Unlike his mother, she was not tolerant of his unfaithfulness. His relationship with his in-laws bordered on complete formality and this brought about marital strain. As Komarovsky (1964) puts it, ''A husband may be less involved with his in-laws because he is less involved with his wife.'' In some strained marriages, the husbands and wives escape into their own families of origin and this seemed true for Alice in both a physical and psychological sense. She visited her own family separately and he saw his in-laws only when necessary. However, he believed that eventually she would realize that he was the only person she had.

As Komarovsky (1964) found in her study of blue collar workers, the authority attached to a husband's status is a major source of his power in many families. This becomes especially visible when the husband takes selfish advantage of his position and the wife accepts frustrations as the normal lot of married women.

John's relationship with his wife continued to deteriorate. Trust was disappearing from the marriage. Unfortunately, trust is not granted as part of a dowry, nor is it built into a legal contract that binds the couple. It is something that is worked at and developed by mutual, conscious effort, often taking two steps forward and one back. John was surprised that his problems continued even after the child was born. He expected his wife to be child-oriented and not to be concerned about his going out with other women. He hoped that his child would provide the reasons for keeping the marriage and family alive and also help in filling the emotional gap between him and his wife. But this did not happen. Tension and friction between them increased. He felt that his wife, who stayed home doing routine work and did not meet new people should be grateful to him for their beautiful child. From John's perspective, the child was conceived with the hope that its presence would mend a fractured marriage. There is a myth in many marriages that indicates the advent of children would automatically improve a difficult or unfulfilled marriage. But the child brought pain instead. The daughter at a young age became the mother's ally. The child's presence in this discordant union only instigated new troubles because of the added responsibilities.

MIDDLE AGE

As time passed, relations became increasingly bitter between John and his wife. He expected her, as a woman to be restrained because they were "nice, respectable people," but she would "scream and shout at him like an animal." One day, to his horror, he discovered that his wife was involved with another man. He could not believe it. She was the "woman of the house" and her role was to maintain the coherence of the family. He stormed out of the house, swearing that he would never return. Thinking in economic terms, this was the second house he had bought out of hard savings and he could not believe that his wife would cheat on him when he provided for her so well. He added that if his wife had not gone to her family with complaints and had not displeased him, he would not have gone out with other women. John was obviously in pain when he talked about his broken dreams. It was almost as if he wished to relive his life and make his marriage work, though he shied away from talking about his own behavior. He decided that he would make Alice suffer, so he did not give her any money, but visited and took his daughter out. It surprised him that he was not pursued for money.

Six long years after his painful separation, his wife sued him for a divorce that he did not wish to give as there was the myth of a long-lasting marriage. Usually, marriage vows contain a pledge of mutual commitment to stay wed "in sickness and in health" and promises about loving, honoring, protecting, and cherishing.

Marriage was entered into seriously and was to last as long as the partners lived. It was expected that when problems and misfortunes arose, the couple would either triumph over them or accept them stoically.

The seeds of marital disruption were sown early in the marriage when Alice and John developed a pattern of physical and emotional distancing (Searles, 1960). John somehow still expected his wife to be faithful based on his family of origin myth that indicated women were weak and needed men. It was a shock to him, when she asked him for a divorce, even after they had lived apart for over six years. It appeared that his wife had already gone through the emotional divorce and he was lagging behind. However, this was not verbalized to me. How could he? Men were strong. John had experienced tremendous disenchantment in the marriage but was grieved to think of divorce.

Irrespective of his negative reactions, his wife went ahead and sued him for divorce and also paid for it, the ultimate destruction of the family myth that women were weak. Then the myth was further shaken when the wife unexpectedly announced her intentions of marrying a dentist. John found out that this dentist was the man who had paid for the divorce. So, he added, he knew that she was a weak person and it was "that man" who made her do it. This dentist was over 15 years older than his wife but she did not seem to mind. Because of the intense tension between John and his former wife, the child was placed in a boarding school. He was allowed to take her home with him every weekend, but after his wife remarried, she took custody of the child and he saw less and less of his daughter. However, he mused, his wife did have a man to take care of her. Family myths are powerful!

What route did John's life take from then on? He went out with a number of women and started to drink too much. He had been drinking heavily even when his wife was there, but now it became excessive. Also he dated incessantly. We talked for a whole session about his "exploits" with women. This included a beautiful, wealthy woman whom he wanted to marry but it did not work out. She was divorced, but her daughters did not want her to remarry. Women are fun, he told me with a twinkle in his eye. But the paradox was that without them he felt lifeless. Eventually, he met the "perfect" woman, Teresa, whom he dated for a few months before they decided to marry. She was beautiful, unlike his wife, had long blonde hair, and was the mother of two gorgeous children. However, less than a year later she was diagnosed as having a cancer and was dead before he could digest the news. It was a horrible shock for him and it took him some time to recover from it.

He missed Teresa and drank excessively, his only coping mechanism. Finally, he fell ill with pneumonia and had to be hospitalized. In the hospital, he met a fabulous looking nurse. She had blonde hair, too, and he wanted to marry her, but she was a strict Catholic and did not wish to marry him because he was divorced. He remembered that he had proposed to her at least 20 times, but she would consistently refuse him. So he did something that was exciting and different. He moved next door to her in the same apartment building and soon they were living together. He has known her for the past 24 years. They have remained the best of friends and she has taken care of him consistently and well. When he had a stroke a few years ago, she made all the arrangements to take him to the hospital. Eventually, he was confined to a wheelchair and she could not take care of him because she was employed full time. Did she ever want to marry? He replied that she did after he got the stroke when he could not move around. He felt that it was more out of a sense of obligation, as she had given him 24 years of her life. At that time, he could not work, he could not take care of her, and he did not have anything to offer her. He added that he would not have been able to manage on his social security money. Omitted from his story until later was the fact that he was not physically mobile to be able to move around. I suspected that he might have some anxiety about his sexual performance but I did not pursue the topic. However, he had been a resident of this institution for the past few years and his woman friend visited him every week. His daughter visited him about once a month or even less often.

How was his relationship with his daughter? He loved her very much. She was an ambitious woman, held an extremely important job, and made a lot of money. His only regret was that she was not married and he felt that his former wife had not allowed that to happen. He described Tina as being tied to his wife's apron strings. Though she was in her forties, she could not date anyone unless Alice approved. He felt that his ex-wife had unduly influenced his daughter to be suspicious of men and he described his daughter as being severe in her dress and makeup. She made good money, however, and was happy to be on her own. On the other hand, Alice's daughter by her second husband (the dentist) was happily married and had two children of her own.

While John viewed all women as weak, his daughter, Tina, who lived with her mother, learned to view all men as untrustworthy. This was directly connected to the fact that John caused Tina and her mother immense pain. The overprotectiveness of the mother towards Tina was seen in the unusual behavior of the mother in scrutinizing her dates. If John considered women as weak, his daughter was a contradiction to this myth and played out the woman's perspective that women were not weak. Perhaps his wife was also a strong woman and it is this contradiction in personality and behaviors that led to the break-up of Alice and John's marriage.

OTHER IMPORTANT ITEMS IN JOHN'S LIFE

One of the most important things in John's life was a cat that he loved very much. He had this cat with him for over 12 years and felt totally lost when it died a year ago. It was a black cat and though he was mostly Irish in his thinking and believed that black cats could bring you bad luck, he was extremely attached to it. After it died, his lady friend bought him another cat which he liked, but it was never the same. He felt that he and his earlier cat understood each other. Human life is not lived out in a vacuum. Experiences of subjective unity with the nonhuman environment have a place in the mature person's life (Searles, 1960). This is because people's basic emotional orientation can be expressed in one word: relatedness. In relatedness there is a sense of intimate kinship, a psychological concomitant to the structural kinship that exists between people and the various ingredients of the person's nonhuman environment. Searles (1960) writes about a patient who maintained a relationship with a dog. This dog provided the individual with companionship and the love and assurance of being needed, which were more easily obtainable from an animal than from people. Similarly, John loved his cat with a relatedness that made him become nurturing and added to the quality of his life.

Sense of Self

John continued that if he had to live his life all over again he would live it differently. He would care more about people and not worry about having fun all his life. After all fun had not taken him too far. The family myth from his family of origin had distorted reality for him and the rest of the family members, but it held them together as a group. However, when he attempted to carry over this family myth to his family of procreation, he was struck with a different reality. All women are not weak and dependent. He was especially conscious of this when he found himself confined to a wheelchair, with a working girlfriend and a very successful working daughter. If there was any awareness of this falsity of the myth, it was not verbalized at any point in the interviews.

What was John's identity at this point? The total set of images one has of oneself is called total identity, made up of a person's aptitudes, capabilities, fears, vulnerabilities and weaknesses, past experiences, moral qualities, social status, and role. A minimal fourfold division recognizes real, ideal, feared, and claimed identities (Boszormenyi-Nagy and Framo, 1965).

A real identity is a subset of images that one believes, privately, to be a true present description of oneself as he or she ''really'' is. Ideal identity is a subset of images that people would like to be able to say was true but which they do not necessarily believe is true at present. The ideal subset of images often includes morally ideal components, which incorporate amoral or even, in relation to local conventions, immoral or negative, in Erikson's sense, identities. An ideal identity could embrace both id-determined and superego-determined fantasies and often is not internally consistent. Feared identity is a subset of images which one would not like to say is true of oneself at present and which the person does not necessarily believe is true of himself or herself. Claimed identity is a subset of images that a person would like another party to believe is his/her real identity (Boszormenyi-Nagy and Framo, 1965). At times, with respect to a given dimension of variation, the real, ideal, feared, and claimed identities can be construed as points on a linear continuum, such as a scale, or as a discrete or continuous variable.

When I was leaving I heard John's words echoing in my ears: "I am a strong person and will always be in charge of myself." I smiled and nodded my head, affirmatively, and as I walked away I realized that it was John's ideal identity talking to me—for the reality was that he was physically (because of his stroke and partial paralysis) and economically dependent upon the agency.

POSTSCRIPT

When I went back to see John after an interval of one and a half years for a follow-up, I found him jubilant. "Perhaps you like me," he flirted. I saw the twinkle in his eyes. He had just turned 73. "I like you," I responded. He had dyed his hair black, which did not go with his elderly looks, and he wore a shirt that was bright and colorful. I chuckled to myself. Old habits die hard. After all, I was a woman and he felt that he could attract me. Of course, it was flattering, too, that he would dress up for a researcher. Do family myths from the family of origin ever die? In the follow-up, I found his memory as good as it was when we first met and the information he had given was accurate from his perspective as he repeated some of the earlier narrative. After two hours of reminiscing with him, through the webs of his life, I left John.

CHAPTER 7

Conclusions and Implications

The utilization of family myths presented in this volume has helped me to understand the complexities of behavior and interactions of families seen in therapy as well as in everyday life. The types of family myths provide the organizing principles and help make sense of the very complicated dynamics with which families operate. Therapists have to grapple with these factors. I have described some aspects of my work with one person in each of several families to illustrate how the stories they present may be seen in part as family myths whose function is to protect and defend shared preoccupations that the family has from conscious awareness to a certain degree. These are derived from myths brought by each partner to the marriage that have constituted a dynamic substratum for the subsequently formed family.

This atypical study of elderly people in an institutional setting had many advantages as well as disadvantages. Being able to focus on a person's life from childhood to old age made it possible to see the tracks of family myths throughout each life. The ability of these individuals to tell the story and to feel some of the same emotions that were experienced as a member of both the family of origin and the family of procreation was remarkable. The powerful influences that the subculture of the family left on these members were also evident. It was useful to understand the theme of the myth of each family from the perspective of each of these different interviewees. The disadvantage that I faced was the lack of observation of the rest of the family members, though in two cases the living spouse was also interviewed.

It would be a mistake to assume that family myths exist just in families who need help. They are present in all kinds of families, performing the function of maintaining the coherence of the family. They have an impact on each individual. Thus, individual behavior and family myths are closely interrelated. In many ways the individual and the family group are two distinguishable parts; yet in their mutual reflections and influences they are part of an inseparable world. Any role an individual plays becomes meaningful in the framework of family relationships.

SUMMARY AND CONCLUSIONS

Emily Crosby's case (Chapter 3) deals with the four-generational family myth that indicates "men are bad and need only sex from women." This family myth separated men from the women in many ways. Women chose weak, alcoholic men for husbands, who then played peripheral roles in the family and were treated as outsiders. Women stayed together tightly knit and this closeness came through their shared anger and negativeness against men.

In Paul Fink's family (Chapter 4), the three-generation family myth indicated that men were psychologically weak and women had to take care of them. Thus family members learned to deny the presence of strength in men.

Though Paul Fink's first wife died of cancer and his second wife killed herself, Paul and his children firmly believed that he was a weak person and needed a woman's support. When Paul in his sixties walked through a snowstorm for hours and survived it, this was ignored. He was a man and viewed as a weak person; only when he remarried for the third time could his children relax.

Melissa Simpson (Chapter 5) reflects the family myth that "We are a happy family." In this family the emphasis was placed on illness. Although Melissa's mother controlled her family through her heart condition, the overall family myth said, "We are a happy family and we do not get angry." Each person had a role to play and lived up to it. Melissa's mother was the "sick" person; the father was the quiet responsible man; Matilda was the home-manager; Leonard was the "fun child"; and Melissa played the role of the "pet" and "bright" child. This maintained the coherence of the family.

When Melissa grew older, she also developed a heart problem and her husband catered to her. Thus, the family myth of the "happy family" sustained by one member's illness was maintained in her family of procreation as well.

John Howard's family history (Chapter 6) deals with a two-generation family myth that indicates, "Women are weak and dependent and should cater to men who would take care of them." This family myth kept women in subordination to men. It appeared to work in John's family of origin. Men consciously chose women who would cater to them. However, in John's marriage the balancing of personalities was not meaningful. His wife got tired of him and his "loose ways" and eventually divorced him. John was convinced that his wife divorced him only because of the influence and help of her lover and friend, a dentist—a MAN. In his mind, she was still a weak woman and only catering to the needs of her male friend.

John's wife mistrusted him and, as a result, their daughter, Tina, who lived with the mother, grew up influenced by another myth that said, "Men should not be trusted." She became an independent career woman and did not marry.

The myth that women were weak and dependent was again not true with John's woman friend who held a job and took care of him. However, John said, "I am a strong person and will always be in charge of myself," even though the reality at that time in his life was that he was physically disabled and economically dependent on the agency.

A family myth could be shaken by events or circumstances, as could individual defenses. When individual defenses are tampered with, the system of family myths in which the individual is involved is also affected. To maintain oneself within the myth, lack of awareness to some degree is a necessary ingredient.

The function of maintaining the family's equilibrium often imposes the self-reinforcement of negative or positive behavioral patterns among individual family members. For instance, John Howard mentioned that he was expected to be like his father who was "handsome looking and played around." John was constantly compared to him and lived up to it. He played around and his marriage broke up. However, he consoled himself: "I was just like my father." Sometimes individuals sacrifice their life goals in order to maintain the balance of the family.

At other times there may be marriages of opposites, as seen in Emily Crosby's case, where the women who were nonalcoholics constantly chose alcoholic men as partners. Here, the extension of the collusive defense of the family is complex. The children get an opportunity to join either parent's camp. Each camp would view its role as ideal and tend to view the other as the flawed one. In Emily's case, her daughters joined her camp and the other parent was scapegoated as the "bad" person. Every family develops its own culture and often there is a clear picture of frozen, dysfunctional disharmony.

The family is an evolving system of interacting relationships; this includes in its structure sensitive areas whose exposure is felt by the family members to be dangerous and threatening to their survival as a unit. To keep a family functioning as a unit, compromises are needed to defend the family against unresolved conflicts and anxiety. Individual family members actively or passively, openly or tacitly, contribute to this defensive system. Every family member experiences some individual need for it as well.

When the family system is rigid, it is difficult to penetrate the avoided areas. By playing the necessary roles, the family members protect the family. In such families, a child often plays the role of the family scapegoat and thus fulfills the family's needs. Parents view children as a way of fulfilling their own needs and expectations. Through the child's birth the parent feels that they have another chance to feel adequate, lovable, needed, strong and complete.

Even when couples are unhappy or find their relationships to each other thorny and painful, and are disillusioned with each other, they may continue to live together for the sake of the "child." The child, on the other hand, feels that the parents have implicitly asked him/her to live for them and that he or she is the important person who has the power, the responsibility, and the mandate to make them happy. Even if a child does not receive such a message, he or she would perform a dysfunctional role like being "ill" or "troublesome" if this would keep the family together for his or her sake.

For example, when a myth is created in a family—such as "We are a happy family," as shown in Melissa's case—this prevents the family members from dealing with their anger towards each other. They live with the constant cover-up that everything is well with the family. Even though the mother has a number of heart attacks and the older daughter runs away from home a number of times, the myth in the family says, "We are a happy family"; anything that is painful is overlooked as if it does not exist. Throughout the interviewing Melissa had a pleasant smile on her face reflecting her sincere belief that she came from a happy family.

Working with information about family myths during therapy, along with other variables such as individual dynamics, family structure, and cultural influences, can serve us well by enlarging our vision and expanding our understanding.

As seen in the families studied, the myth represents a compromise from which every family member gets satisfaction, however meager it may be. The myth is more dominant in some families than in others as the foundation of family life. Thomas Mann (1936) might have had the family group in mind when he spoke of the myth as the tireless schema, the pious formula into which life flows when it reproduces its traits out of consciousness. The family myth is accepted by all family members as a group and it is a shared group image which each member appears to carry with him or her.

Following are some of the major types of myths found in this study (see pp. 9–10):

Myth of harmony
Myth of the family scapegoat
Myth of catastrophism
Myth of pseudomutuality
Myth of overgeneralization
Myth of togetherness
Myth of salvation and redemption

All the cases in this study exhibited the influence of one or more of these myths.

TOXIC AND LESS TOXIC MYTHS

It became apparent that myths could be classified as toxic and less toxic. Family myths are more or less articulate and they are internally consistent (Stierlin, 1973a). These myths might be presented as tightly reasoned stories, explicit creeds, or vaguely formulated assumptions. They are collaborative formulations on the part of the family which serve to dilute or deny the formidable reality of past and present family involvements. The vagueness of these formulations could reflect a low level of ego integration and articulation in different family members and in the family system as a whole. This could represent a joint strategy for obscuring and overlooking painful conflicts and confrontations between family members (Stierlin, 1973a). This was seen in Melissa's case where there were no meaningful confrontations, but rather a constant denial of feelings.

Family members are constantly aware of less toxic myths but they are viewed as taboos. They are half-truths, simplifications of reality organized in an objective manner to help maintain the family. In the Fink family, there is an awareness of homosexuality in the family, but it is viewed as taboo and made into a family secret. In less toxic myths, the defenses are to some extent conscious and mingled with the desire to sustain the family as a system. Although there is some awareness that the problem exists it is unacceptable to openly acknowledge it. To do so would be viewed as damaging or even catastrophic; therefore, the tendency is to keep it a secret.

In toxic myths there is total unawareness, because they are utilized unconsciously and blindly in the family. In such myths, there is an unconscious, shared fantasy that is connected with an avoided theme. The purpose of this unconscious theme is to form a group system of defenses protecting different areas of vulnerability and unacknowledged conflict among family members. In such families, the family system is rigid and the avoided areas are loaded with negatives that are impervious to penetration. This inability to acknowledge problems also plays an important role in family relationships and dynamics. These myths safeguard the family members' involvement with each other as they continue their family drama while wearing masks. The shared fantasy in Paul Fink's family says, "Men are all weak."

There is an instrumental value to the toxic or less toxic family myth as well. It says, "This is the way we are. Accept us as such and do not question us." It is an example of a living cliché, an animated album of family pictures, as Ferreira (1963) puts it, that nobody dares to erase or throw away; they are essential to the legimatization and consecration of an ongoing relationship. At times, the family myth may, on the surface, be focused predominately on an individual. However, emotional forces involve the whole family of relationships. A classical symptom seen in families is an obsession with drinking; another myth encompasses the suicidal gestures by some family members that are viewed not just in terms of the individual, but also as aspects of the particular relationship within which they occur. These symptoms become susceptible to having a greater and richer significance for families.

FAMILY THERMOSTAT

As Ferreira (1963) notes, family myths have a survival value as well. In many families the myth functions as a family thermostat and is brought into function by the emotional temperature of the family. Every family has its thermostat set at a temperature that is comfortable for its own affective functioning. For the Crosby family, negative mechanisms are a part of family functioning. With evasions, denials, double messages, threats, and bribes, the family is back to its original patterns of interaction. Thus the thermostat attempts to maintain the status quo or re-establish the family's previous steady state.

Family myths increase in significance when negative tensions reach predetermined thresholds among family members or threaten to disrupt relationships that are either real or fantasized. The family thermostat regulates the family temperature and attempts to control any family mishap. Like any coherence factor, the myth keeps the family from being damaged or destroying itself. Just as individuals utilize defenses to protect themselves, so do families utilize the myth to defend and protect the family homeostasis.

One might view the family thermostat as set at three levels of temperature: high temperature (hot), very low temperature (freezing), or medium. Depending on the type of family, any one of these temperature levels could have a stabilizing effect on the family by maintaining the state of coherence or balance that is comfortable for the members. Hot temperature families are emotionally involved (fused) with each other completely, as seen in the Crosby household. There is not much differentiation and the home atmosphere is full of negative myths that sustain the emotional conflict, anger and fears. Family scapegoating, collusions, and emotionally volatile situations are ever present, keeping the family stuck together because of individual members' own needs. Cold temperature families maintain myths that encourage distancing. Discussions about feelings are limited or superficial; disagreements or anger are rarely expressed. Melissa Simpson's family came close to this type of family and the theme, ''We are a happy family,'' was constantly presented. Taboos and secrets may be part of both cold and hot temperature families and there is the presence of pseudomutuality among both these types of families.

The midtemperature families are the so-called ''normal'' families with a number of myths that are both positive and negative. They are more reality-oriented and accomplish their family tasks, particularly the successful development of offspring and the ability to function meaningfully in society.

The family myth protects the family against the threat of disintegration and chaos. It also aims at increasing the level of organization in the family by establishing patterns that perpetuate themselves with the circularity and self-correction characteristic of any homeostatic mechanism. The family members constantly derive satisfaction from the myth regardless of the reality of the situation. When a myth, is constantly repeated, like "We are a happy family," it permits the individual to accept the family at face value and without challenge.

IMPLICATIONS

An important implication is that family myths can sometimes be shaken by events or circumstances just as individual defenses can be shaken. In order to maintain the family myth, a certain degree of "insightlessness" is necessary. Maintaining the myth is part of a struggle to maintain a relationship that is obviously experienced as vital and necessary to keep the family functioning as a unit. To maintain the coherence of the family, the myth imposes the self-reinforcement of the behavior of individual family members, as seen in John Howard's family where the myth had it that John was "cute and playful" as a young man—a replica of his father. John continued to be "cute and playful" even after his marriage because this notion was reinforced in his family of origin. John mentioned that he took pride in his behavior even though his marriage ended in divorce. After his divorce, he continued to have what seemed like an overly active social and sexual life. How much did John enjoy this behavior and how much did he suffer from it? We do not know. However, these examples show that family myths and individual behavior in families go hand in hand.

Thus, family myths bring two factors together—the intrapsychic content and the interpersonal interaction produced from the system of role images that people create for themselves in families. The family images have been studied only through the pathways of family myths in the life of an individual. This study revealed that the family group was an integral part of the person's thoughts, feelings and behavior.

If the hypothesis is correct that consensus role images are required by families in order to live together, then it has important implications for working with families who are extruding one or more members from the household.

All family myths fulfill protective and defensive functions. On the intrafamily level they defend the members against painful confrontations with aspects of real past and present involvements with each other. In relation with the outside world they prevent intrusions and unsettling judgments. This provides family members with a sense of relief and security in maintaining their own coherence and balance in the family.

The 25 cases studied revealed some of the major myths present in families. The four detailed case studies revealed the different types of myths present in four lower-class families. The people who were interviewed were elderly, and had maintained firm beliefs in their own family myths, over a long period of time—a lifetime, in effect.

What value does this have for family therapy purposes? The family therapist must bear in mind that myths are held on to as long as they are needed, even if it takes two or more generations as we saw in the case of Emily Crosby (Chapter 3).

Another important implication is that even though family myths perform the important function of defending the family and holding it together as long as necessary, the therapist should attempt to work at these myths that control the family if they are detrimental to its functioning.

As the therapist challenges the family myths, he or she must provide family members with a model and a framework for safe exploration of their interpersonal accounts. As suggested by Boszormenyi-Nagy and Spark (1973), the therapist has to do this with fairness, empathy, and integrity.

All family myths have a justifying and validating rather than an explanatory function. The purpose of a family myth is to provide a rationale for family members' behavior.

When children grow up and get married, they need to deal with conflicting myths that may be present from two different homes. The old beliefs need to be altered to fit a new family and its own evolving norms and rules of behavior.

Family myths protect the family from facing reality as it is and binds anxiety. They also function as a social facade and as a family's defense mechanism. Family members may collude to distort their family reality so as to avoid dealing with pain or conflict. They do this through denial or rationalization about what they have or have not done to each other in the family. For instance, in Melissa Simpson's family one child was overworked; when she complained, her mother told her to cut her long, beautiful, blonde hair. This daughter was obviously unhappy, but the family learned to tell outsiders, "We are a happy family." This served the function of placing the negative behavior in a context that did not threaten the coherence of the family.

Families create smoke screens by which they keep outsiders confused and ignorant about the family's real involvements. In such situations family members do not have to face painful confrontations which would spell family disintegration and chaos. Myths protect families from outsiders. Families who feel they have something to hide view outsiders, including family therapists, as intruders who wish to enter the family without the family's permission and cause them pain and embarrassment. They fear that any kind of public exposure would open old accounts and wounds and elicit guilt and shame. So it was in Paul Fink's family where the brother's homosexuality was viewed as taboo and kept secret from outsiders.

Family myths are also used where adult and young members at times compromise their behavior and potential to fit a family system. The compromise appears in the form of family myths—a parent who is an alcoholic or one who has a large number of "heart attacks." These compromises are created and maintained from within as a way of avoiding reality as it is. I observed that disturbed families have an amazing capacity to induce collusive denial systems. Different family members rotate around roles that are specifically required by the family.

The therapist has to be an impartial arbiter and investigator in exploring the various members' involvements with each other. By focusing on these intrafamilial transactions, the therapist can point up the fallacies underlying the myths that are proffered. He or she can identify the hostilities that underlie a professed myth of harmony. Or instead of pinpointing these discrepancies the therapist may create an atmosphere of exploration which allows myths to die a natural death. In such situations, the therapist has to adopt a multigenerational perspective which widens the scope within which accounts are assessed. For instance, how can one do justice to a schizophrenic mother who dumps her anger on her child and associates all her dissociated anger with that child's behavior unless the therapist takes into account the mother's family of origin? It is important to remember that the family transactions give rise to those relational patterns that are transferred, inappropriately and repetitively, to nonfamily contexts. Myths are, in a way, straightjackets that keep relational patterns locked up within the family system, preventing them from being pried loose and seen as they really are.

Myths, in summary, appear to safeguard the family members' entrenchment and involvement with each other. Instead of being windows through which the therapist may look at a family's interior, they distract the therapist from what is real and keep the outsider really outside.

This study is a beginning of a journey. There are many unexplored areas that would be relevant for future studies. Individuals and families belonging to different cultures and socioeconomic classes need to be studied. It would be valuable to see how age and sex differences affect the development and use of myths. What seems clear is that it is necessary to understand family myths in order to comprehend family relationships.

Appendix

INTERVIEW GUIDE

1. *Name (optional).*
2. *Age.*
   60–64
   65–69
   70–74
   75–79
   80–84
   85
3. *Sex.*
   Male
   Female
4. *Marital status.*
   Married, widowed, divorced, separated, remarried, single.
5. *Occupation before retirement.*
   White collar, Blue collar.
6. *Annual income.*
   Below $5000
   $5,001–10,000
   $10,001–15,000
   $15,001–20,000

$20,001–25,000
$25,001–30,000
$30,001–35,000
$35,001–45,000
$45,001+

7. *Former living arrangements.*
   Type of housing
   Own house
   Rented house
   Condo

8. *Length of stay in present institution.*
   1–5 years
   6–10 years
   11–15 years
   16–20 years
   20+

9. *If married, number of children.*
   0
   1–2
   3–4
   5–6
   7+

10. *Number of sons and daughters.*
    Sons
    Daughters

11. *Number of children living at present.*

12. *How long were/are you married?*
    21–30 years
    31–40 years
    41–50 years
    51–60 years
    61+

13. *If married more than once, specify the number of years you were married to each spouse.*

14. What were your ideas about marriage?

15. Did you believe that you should do everything together in your social life?

16. Did you believe that once you were married most of your problems would be solved?
    Why?
17. Did you believe that you should have no secrets from each other?
    Yes/no/not sure.
    Did you, in fact, keep secrets from your spouse?
18. Did you believe that you should not quarrel with each other at any time?
    Yes/no/not sure.
19. How often did you quarrel (more or less)?
    Frequently/occasionally/rarely.
20. What were your chief reasons for quarreling?
    Inlaws, children, sex, each other, other reasons.
21. Did you believe that good sexual relationships would result in a good marriage?
    Yes/no/not sure.
    Why?
22. Did you believe that extramarital relations would help make a marriage last longer or would extramarital relations break a marriage?
    Yes/no/not sure.
23. Who was the really "good one" between you and your spouse?
    You/your spouse/both/none.
    Why?
24. On reflection, would you view your family life as happy?
25. Did you at any time believe that if you had problems in your marriage children would hold it together?
    Yes/no/not sure.
    Why?
26. What was considered most "sacred" in your family?
    Why?
27. Did you follow any rituals in your family? Why?
28. What type of family image did you present to outsiders?
29. Was this image true in the family itself?
    Yes/no/not sure.

30. Was the image an accurate one for the family as a whole or for individual family members?
31. With reference to your first spouse, how loving was he/she?
32. How responsible was he or she?
33. Who was the "bad" one in the family?
    Why?
34. In what ways do your children resemble your last spouse?
35. In your opinion, how happy, unhappy, or fairly happy were you with that spouse?
    Why?
36. Did you originally believe that having a child meant that you had someone to love you?
    Is this true completely, partially, not at all.
    Why?
37. How did you view children in your family?
    Child no. 1, 2, 3, 4, 5, 6, 7, 8, 9.
    The best child
    The happy child
    The funloving child
    The troublemaker
    The sly one
    The pest
    The complainer
    The black sheep
38. At this point in your life, do these images still hold true?
    Yes/no.
    Why?
39. Did you view your children as your second chance to achieve your goals in life?
    Yes/no.
    If yes, how did it happen?
40. What were your reasons for having children?
41. What do you believe your children owe you?
    Love/respect/obedience/anything else?
    Why?
42. Did your children meet your expectations and your needs?
    At all times/sometimes/never. Why?

43. Did family members play different roles, such as the one member who was always smiling and never bothered by anything? Or the one who would lose his or her temper at the slightest provocation?
44. Which child was called the "wild one" and which one was called the "quiet one"? As children grew older, did they exchange roles?
45. Who was the head of the family?
    Mother/father/elder son/daughter/spouse's mother/spouse's father/your father/your mother.
46. Was there any member in the family who was constantly sick? If yes, why?
47. Who took care of that person?
48. Were there any rules regarding how this person should be cared for, in the family?
    Yes/no. Why?
49. Would you consider anyone in the family as bad or totally negative?
    If yes, why?
50. As a young parent, who was your favorite child?
    1, 2, 3, 4, 5, 6, 7, 8, 9.
    Why?
51. Who is your favorite child now?
    The same/different/none.
52. Do you believe that the ideas you had about your children still hold true? That is, the happy child is still the happy child.
    Yes/no.
    Why?
53. Do you believe that as parents get older children should take care of them? What are your reasons for feeling this way?
54. Have your children retained their attitude of love and respect towards you?
    Yes/no.
    Why?
55. Did you and your spouse like the same children?
    Yes/no. Why?

56. If your children had a problem, would they go to your spouse or would they go to you?
    Why?
57. Who were the extended family members who played a role in your life?
    Your spouse's mother, your spouse's father, both.
58. Did you like your inlaws?
    Yes/no.
59. How would you describe them?
    Decent, interfering, destructive, okay.
    Why?
60. How did your parents view your spouse?
    Did you agree with them?
    Yes/no. Why?
61. Did their opinions of your spouse influence your attitude towards him or her?
62. Why and to what extent?
63. How did inlaws view you?
64. In your opinion, was your spouse influenced by this attitude of your parents? Why?
65. What roles did inlaws play in your marriage?
    Very involved, somewhat involved, indifferent. Why?
66. How did your parents view you?
67. Did this image hold true for you as you grew older?
    Yes/no. Why?
68. How were your siblings viewed by your parents?
69. Would you consider your own family as being similar to your parents' family?
    Yes/no. Why?
70. Whom do your grandchildren resemble?
71. Do your grandchildren's behavior reflect your behavior/your spouse's?
    Yes/no. Why?

Is there any special incident you wish to relate about any family member who was constantly getting into trouble, was always helpful, etc.? Please do so. If you have questions, feel free to ask me.

Thank you.

References

Barnard, C. P. and Corrales, R. C. *The Theory and Technique of Family Therapy.* Springfield, IL: Charles C Thomas, 1979.

Bateson, G. *Mind and Nature.* New York: Dutton, 1979.

Bentovim, A., Barnes, G. G. and Cooklin, A. (Eds.). *Family Therapy, Vol. 2.* New York: Grune and Stratton, 1982.

Boatright, M. C., Downs, R. B., and Flanagan, J. T. *The Family Saga.* Champaign, IL: University of Illinois, 1958.

Boszormenyi-Nagy, I. A theory of relationships: Experiences and transaction. In I. Boszormenyi-Nagy and J. Framo (Eds.), *Intensive Family Therapy.* New York: Harper and Row, 1965 (a).

Boszormenyi-Nagy, I. Intensive family therapy as a process. In I. Boszormenyi-Nagy and J. Framo (Eds.), *Intensive Family Therapy.* New York: Harper and Row, 1965(b).

Boszormenyi-Nagy, I. and Framo, J. (Eds.) *Intensive Family Therapy.* New York: Harper and Row, 1965. (New Edition: Brunner/Mazel, 1985).

Boszormenyi-Nagy, I. and Spark G. *Invisible Loyalties.* New York: Harper and Row, 1973 (New Edition: Brunner/Mazel, 1984).

Bott, E. *Family and Social Networks.* London: Tavistock 1957.

Bowen, M. Theory in the practice of psychotherapy. In P. J. Guerin (Ed.), *Family Therapy.* New York: Gardner Press, 1976.

Bowen, M. *Clinical Practice in Family Therapy.* New York: Jason Aronson, 1978.

Box, S. J. The elucidation of a family myth. *Journal of Family Therapy,* 1979, *1,* 75–86.

Brunvard, H. *The Study of American Folklore.* New York: Norton, 1978.

Byng-Hall, J. Family myths used as defense in conjoint family therapy. *British Journal of Medical Psychology,* 1973, *46,* 239–250.

Carter, E. A. and McGoldrick, M. The family life cycle. In F. Walsh (Ed.), *Normal Family Processes.* New York: Guilford Press, 1982.

Cox, T. *Stress*. Baltimore: University Park Press, 1978.

Crandall, R. C. *Gerontology. A Behavioral Science Approach*. Reading, MA: Addison-Wesley, 1969.

Craven, P. and Wellman, B. The network city. *Sociological Inquiry*, 1973, 43 (3 and 4) 57–88.

Dean, B. *The Many Worlds of Dance*. Sydney: Murray Publishing, 1981.

Dicks, H. V. *Marital Tensions: Clinical Studies Toward a Psychological Theory of Interaction*. New York: Routledge and Kegan Paul, 1967.

Dilthey, W. (Ed.) *Pattern and Meaning in History*. New York: Harper and Row, 1962.

Dundes, A. *The Study of Folklore*, New Jersey: Prentice-Hall, 1965.

Edward, J., Ruskin, N. and Turrini, P. *Separation and Individualization*. New York: Gardner Press, 1981.

Erikson, E. H. *Identity and the Life Cycle*. New York: Norton, 1959.

Ferreira, A. J. Family myth and homeostasis. *Archives of General Psychiatry*, 1963, 9, 457–463.

Ford, F. R. Rules: The invisible family. *Family Process*, 1983, 22(2), 135–145.

Frazer, J. G. *Scapegoat*. New York: Macmillan, 1920.

Goffman, E. *Stigma*. New York: Prentice-Hall, 1963.

Goldenberg, L. and Goldenberg, H. *Family Therapy: An Overview*. Monterey, CA: Brooks/Cole, 1980.

Guerin, P. J. (Ed.) *Family Therapy*. New York: Gardner Press, 1976.

Haley, J. *Strategies of Psychotherapy*. New York: Grune and Stratton, 1964.

Haley, J. *Problem Solving Therapy*. New York: Harper and Row, 1978.

Haskell, A. L. *The Wonderful World of Dance*. New York: Doubleday, 1969.

Henry, J. *Pathways to Madness*. New York: Random House, 1965.

Hoffman, L. *Foundations of Family Therapy*. New York: Basic Books, 1981.

Kantor, D. and Lehr, W. *Inside the Family*. San Francisco: Jossey-Bass, 1975.

Karpel, M. A. Family secrets: Conceptual and ethical issues in relational context. Ethical and practical considerations in therapeutic management. *Family Process*, 1980, 19, 295–306.

Karpel, M. A. and Strauss, E. S. *Family Evaluation*. New York: Gardner Press, 1983.

Komarovsky, M. *Blue Collar Marriage*. New York: Random House, 1964.

Lederer, W. J. and Jackson, D. D. *The Mirages of Marriage*. New York: Norton, 1968.

Levinson, D. J. *The Seasons of a Man's Life*. New York: Knopf, 1978.

Lieberman, S. Nineteen cases of morbid grief. *British Journal of Psychiatry*, 1978, 132, 159–170.

Lindemann, E. The symptomatology and management of acute grief. *American Journal of Psychiatry*, 1949, 101, 141–149.

Mann, T. Freud and the future. *Saturday Review*, 1936, 14, 3–4.

Minuchin, S. *Families and Family Therapy*. Cambridge, MA: Harvard University Press, 1974.

Minuchin, S. and Fishman, H. C. *Family Therapy Techniques*. Cambridge, MA: Harvard University Press, 1982.

Ohmann, R. M. *The Making of the Myth*. New York: Putnam & Sons, 1962.

Okun, B. E. and Rappaport, L. J. *Working with Families*. Mass: Duxbury Press, 1980.

Olson, D. and Sprenkle, D. Emerging trends in treating relationships. *Journal of Marriage and Family Counseling*, 1976, 2(4), 317–329.

Parkes, M. *Bereavement: Studies of Grief in Adult Life*. London: Tavistock, 1972.

Parsons, T. *Social Structure and Personality*. New York: Free Press, 1970.

Sager, C. J. *Marriage Contracts and Couple Therapy*. New York: Brunner/Mazel, 1976.

Searles, H. F. *The Nonhuman Environment*. New York: International Universities Press, 1960.

Skynner, A. C. Indications and counterindications for conjoint family therapy. *International Journal of Social Psychiatry, 1969, 15,* 245–249.

Spiegel, J. P. The resolution of role conflict within the family. In N. Bell and E. F. Vogel (Eds.), *A Modern Introduction to the Family*. Glencoe: The Free Press, 1960.

Stierlin, H. Group fantasies and family myths. Some theoretical and practical aspects. *Family Process*, June, 1973a, 12(2), 111–125.

Stierlin, H. Interpersonal aspects of internalizations. *International Journal of Psychoanalysis*, 1973b, 54.

Sullivan, H. S. *Clinical Studies in Psychiatry*. New York: Norton, 1956.

Sutton-Smith, B., Rosenberg, B. G., and Morgan, E. F. Development of sex differences in choices during preadolescence, *Child Development*, June, 1972, 42, 567–578.

Watzlawick, P. and Weakland, J. H. *The Interactional View*. New York: Norton, 1977.

Weakland, J. Communication theory and clinical change. In P. J. Guerin (Ed.), *Family Therapy*, New York: Gardner Press, 1976.

Willi, J. *Couples in Collusion*. New York: Jason Aronson, 1982.

Wynne, L. C., Ryckoff, I. M., Day, J. and Hirsch, S. I. Pseudomutuality in the family relations of schizophrenics. *Psychiatry*, 1958, 21, 205–220.

Zeitlin, S. J., Kotlin, A. J., and Baker, A. C. (Eds.) *A Celebration of American Folklore*, New York: Pantheon, 1982.

Zuk, G. H. *Family Therapy*. New York: Human Sciences Press, 1981.

Index